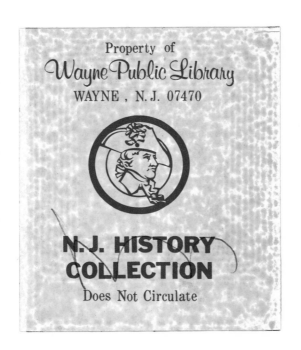

The World Turned Upside Down:
The Story of the American Revolution

About the Book

When the British army under Lord Cornwallis surrendered to American and French forces in 1781, bringing a virtual end to the Revolutionary War, the English band played a tune called "The World Turned Upside Down." Indeed the world had turned so, and never again would be quite the same. In this gripping narrative, historian Robert Leckie tells the story of the Revolution from its causes through the Battle of Yorktown. If it were not all true, it would read like fiction. Here bands of men from low and high places in colonial society pit themselves against the most powerful armies in the world. Skillfully Mr. Leckie focuses on heroes and cowards, wise men and fools on both sides of the Atlantic as the rebels lose and lose, but always return to fight again until a new nation is born.

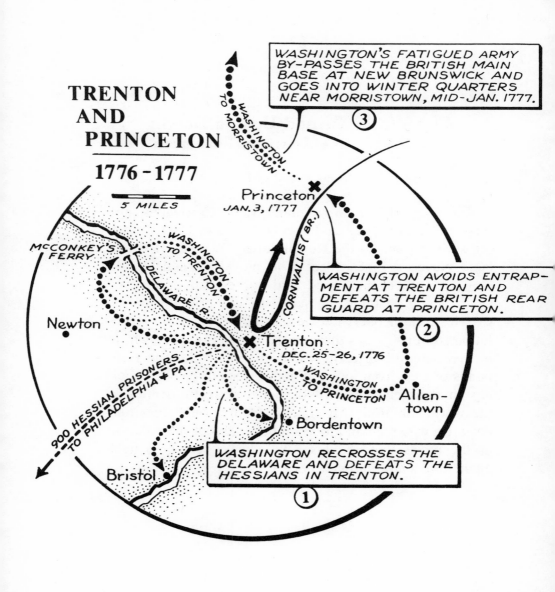

The World Turned Upside Down

The Story of the
American Revolution

by ROBERT LECKIE

With maps by Theodore R. Miller

G. P. Putnam's Sons New York

To all the "Hinder Kinder"
at The Sportsman's Club

Contents

The World Turned Upside Down:
The Story of the American Revolution

1

Rule, Britannia

In the fourteenth century, firearms were invented. In
the fifteenth century, vastly improved navigation tech-
niques opened the world to the sailing ships of Europe—
and Columbus discovered America. Thus, in the six-
teenth century, with guns in one hand and compasses in
the other, the sea powers of Europe began the long
struggle for colonial supremacy that ended in 1763 with
England triumphant.

By the Peace of Paris which ended the Seven Years'
War, England became the world's foremost sea and
colonial power. Its enemies, France and Spain, had been
decisively defeated. Britannia ruled the waves. It possessed colonies and bases on four continents. Its flag flew
over the entire eastern third of the North American con-
tinent. And of all these jewels of empire, the fairest gems

in the imperial crown were the thirteen seaboard colonies of America.

From them, the mother country expected the highest rewards. From them, King George III was confident of receiving the steadiest loyalty and the deepest gratitude. Had not British arms ended the French menace to the north of the colonies and the Spanish threat to the south? Had not the British navy extended the protection of its guns to their commerce? Surely, King George and his ministers reasoned, these colonies which had profited as much as the mother country from her success in war would be willing to pay their share of the cost of waging it.

But they would not.

2

The Quarrel Begins

During the 150 years in which England struggled against France and Spain in the New World, the American colonists had developed a spirit of independence that was unique. They were far freer than colonists living under French or Spanish or Portuguese or Dutch rule.

Each of the thirteen colonies was, in effect, a tiny maritime republic. With varying degrees of self-rule, each ran its own affairs. Each possessed its own Parliament—called House of Burgesses, or House of Delegates, and so forth—which was a miniature replica of Britain's House of Commons. These houses could make laws for the colonies.

True enough, this was not the state of affairs intended by the king and cabinet which governed England, subject to the approval of Parliament. The British crown and the dozen or so ministers who made up the British cabinet had hoped to make the colonies answerable to themselves. This was to be done through the presence of British officials in America. Over the years, however, these magistrates, living 3,000 miles away from king and cabinet, gradually became subject to the strong will of the colonists, who were, after all, their neighbors. So the colonies became more and more independent, at least in internal affairs. They had nothing to say about foreign affairs—that is, the regulation of their relations with other countries or the waging of war against them. This was done by the British Empire itself, of which they were only a part. Thus, they accepted whatever London—the capital of the Empire—might decree on the regulation of their maritime commerce. When London called them to arms, they dutifully went to war against the French in Canada, or, less frequently, the Spanish in Florida. American colonials fought with General James Wolfe when he captured Quebec in the battle that won Canada for England. Before then, they had even mounted expeditions of their own against the French, and these campaigns helped harden their habit of independence. In them, the colonials learned how to wage war independently—that is, how to organize armies and raise the funds necessary to keep them fighting.

In 1763, then, the year of the Peace of Paris, the American colonists were not the dutiful, docile, distant cousins that King George and his ministers believed them to be. Instead, they were probably the most fiercely independent men on earth. And their resentment of British policy—made by men who had never been to America—was already growing.

They distrusted the continued presence of British soldiers in America. True enough, these regulars had been employed to end the French menace in Canada and to suppress the Indian uprising on the western borders known as Pontiac's War. But Canada was now British, and the Indians were all but defeated. Why, then, did the redcoats remain in America? To this, London might reply that they were needed to assist British customs officers, but the colonials thought differently. Privately, they believed that the military garrison was really intended to assert the rights of the crown over the colonies. Publicly, of course, the colonists said nothing—just as they kept their resentment of the Proclamation of 1763 to themselves.

This edict—actually a humane attempt to end the bloody conflict between Indians and white men—closed the vast lands between the Appalachian Mountains and the Mississippi River to the colonists. It reserved this territory for the Indians. Thus, the crown hoped to end the seizure of hunting grounds and villages which was the red man's chief cause of hatred for the whites.

The colonials, however, saw in the proclamation a typically arrogant attempt by British politicians to meddle in their internal affairs. They regarded it as a move to confine them to the eastern seaboard, where they would continue to produce raw materials for Britain and to consume British finished goods. In other words, they were to enter a kind of economic bondage. The thirteen colonies were to be dutiful daughters who would do exactly as they were told for the benefit of the mother country. Meanwhile, their dreams of expansion and improvement were to be shattered, and their children were to be denied their aspirations to possess fine homesteads of their own somewhere "on the waters of the Mississippi." Here, then, was another source of that slowly smoldering resentment, which, fanned into flame, was to lead eventually to rift and rebellion.

Indeed, the battle cry of the Revolution had already been raised publicly. In 1761, in Boston, the lawyer James Otis had electrified a courtroom with the words "Taxation without representation is tyranny!" Up until that moment, there had been no real public outcry against the crown. The colonists still thought of themselves as loyal Englishmen. They had no grievance against Parliament because that august body had not yet attempted to tax them, as it did tax British subjects at home in England. But Otis had laid down the basic challenge to Parliament's right to make laws for the entire empire.

Here was the fundamentally *American* belief that they, and they alone, had the right to tax themselves. Because they had elected no representatives to Parliament, then Parliament could not tax them. To King George and his cabinet and most of Parliament, this was a terrible and treacherous novelty. It threatened the unity of the entire empire. Of course, the colonists were represented, they said. Parliament represented all Englishmen everywhere. No, the colonies replied. It did not. The men in Parliament were Englishmen elected in England, and by a scant 250,000 voters at that. Therefore, again, because the colonies had sent no one to London, London could not tax them. And so, in that glorious year of 1763, when the seas of the world were an English lake, when the roar of the British lion could make men tremble everywhere, on this side of the Atlantic the colonies had set their faces against taxes from abroad, and on the other side the mother country had set her heart on imposing them.

The first attempt to compel the colonies to share the cost of the Empire was the Sugar Act passed in 1764. It replaced the old Molasses Act of 1733, and because it merely raised the existing duty on sugar and other levies, while cutting the molasses tax in half, it would seem to have been acceptable. However, England had been very lax in enforcing the old law, and the colonials had become very skillful in evading it. But this new levy, London made clear, would be *collected*. This meant that the price of rum, which was distilled from molasses and which was the colonials' most popular drink, would go higher. Angry, the colonists vowed that they would not pay the tax.

Worse, the Sugar Act seemed to them to be an unjust tax imposed from abroad. It was not merely the sort of customs duty to which they had no objection. No. In its preamble, the Sugar Act specifically stated that it was intended to help pay the costs of "defending, protecting and securing" America. To London, this seemed fair indeed. Certainly the Americans could not deny the fact that the costs of evicting the French from Canada and suppressing Pontiac had been enormous. The Americans, however, so far from being grateful for this undeniable service, saw the attempt to make them share the costs of it as an outright *taxing* measure. This they would not accept. Once again, the forthright James Otis challenged Parliament's very *right* to tax the colonies. As chairman of a committee of the Massachusetts House of Representatives, he declared that such laws "have a tendency to deprive the Colonies of some of their most essential Rights as British Subjects, and . . . particularly the Right of assessing their own Taxes."

Now the colonies remembered Otis' challenging cry, "Taxation without representation is tryanny!" That remark went echoing publicly through the streets of America. In Boston, a skillful propagandist named Samuel Adams was especially adept at fanning the flames of hatred against Parliament. As yet, no one spoke a word of criticism of King George. It was Parliament, and Parliament alone, that was the culprit. And so, the colonials kept their word: They did not pay the tax. They simply evaded it by smuggling.

A year later, still determined to make the colonies share the costs of empire, Britain imposed the Stamp Act. The colonists were to be compelled to purchase revenue stamps to be affixed to all legal documents, commercial paper, titles, ship charters, bills of lading, newspapers, pamphlets, and playing cards. This, of course, was no more than what was already being done at home in England. But the colonials were furious. It was another *tax*, and they would not pay this one either.

In Virginia a backcountry lawyer named Patrick Henry arose in the House of Burgesses to offer seven resolutions attacking the mother country's right to tax the colonies. The last two of these urged disobedience to the Stamp Act and declared that anyone who obeyed them was an enemy of Virginia. Then, in that bold and ringing style of oratory for which he was already celebrated, Patrick Henry publicly warned King George of the bloody fate that had overtaken other rulers such as Julius Caesar and King Charles I. From somewhere in the chamber there rose the cry of "Treason!" Patrick Henry halted. To this day, it is not known for certain how he replied to the charge. One legend states that he snorted: "If this be treason, make the most of it." Another claims that he quickly apologized to the Speaker and swore that he was ready to die for the king. Whatever Patrick Henry's reply, his famous Virginia Resolves set the entire American seaboard aflame with protests against the Stamp Act.

Even though the most inflammatory of the resolves were not adopted by the Burgesses, it was mistakenly reported that they had been—and the other colonies quickly passed similar resolutions. London was deluged with demands for repeal of the Stamp Act. Moreover, at the request of Massachusetts, a Stamp Act Congress of colonial delegates was held in New York. Nine of the colonies were represented, and the other four probably would have sent deputies of their own, had their assemblies been in session. Expressing their loyalty to the crown, the delegates nevertheless reaffirmed the American belief that Parliament had no right to tax the colonies.

Meanwhile, the detested stamps went unsold. In Georgia, a colony with special obligations to the crown, a few stamps were bought to clear ships from Savannah Harbor. But a rising rumble of protest against even this token purchase swiftly drove the stamp distributor from the colony. North of Georgia, not a stamp was sold. Associations called the Sons of Liberty boarded newly arrived vessels to seize the stamps and destroy them. Stamp officers were forced to resign. Up and down the coast, from Maine to South Carolina, police, judges, lawyers, clergymen and elected officials stood idly by while mobs looted or wrecked the homes of stamp officers or others who spoke out in defense of British authority. Even the governors of the colonies were afraid to move against the rioters. In New Jersey, Maryland, and Massachusetts the governors considered using British soldiers to restore obedience but eventually changed their minds.

And so, as the Stamp Act went unenforced and British authority was roundly flouted, the colonies opened economic warfare. They organized a boycott of British goods. The chief consumers of British products, they refused to buy any more of them. Here they were even more successful. With British factories closed and British workers unemployed, the country's manufacturers appealed to Parliament to repeal the Stamp Act. Parliament complied. A new ministry had come to power in

Britain. It was not as ill disposed toward the colonies as the outgoing one. Moreover, there were members of Parliament who sympathized with the Americans. These factors, together with the weight of the manufacturer's appeal, induced Britain to repeal the Stamp Act. Nevertheless, to save face, Parliament declared that it still had the *right* to pass such laws.

With this, peace returned to the colonies. Overjoyed, the Americans made haste to express their gratitude and loyalty toward the mother country. Sailors, farmers, and mechanics celebrated the "victory" with barrels of beer. Merchants and magistrates toasted King George in goblets of Madeira. Clergymen offered prayers of thanksgiving, and newspapers proclaimed the "victory" of justice over injustice. Thus happy and satisfied, the colonies continued in this tranquil state for about a year—until 1767, when Charles Townshend took over the leadership of Britain.

Here was a man who typified Old World arrogance toward the New. Here was a politician who firmly believed he "understood" the Americans, although he had never crossed the sea to mingle with them. Like so many Europeans of his time, he regarded all colonials as naturally inferior. In those days, there were even scientists who could claim that European animals were superior to American ones. If the extreme heat of the New World did not make creatures lazy, then the iron winters made them slow. So great a literary giant as Dr. Samuel Johnson could describe the Americans as "a race of convicts," and there does not seem to be any doubt that leaders

21

such as Charles Townshend agreed with him. Moreover, when Townshend came to power, the wealthy classes of Britain had begun to protest against rising taxes and to complain that the prosperous Americans were not made to pay their share.

Thus supported, Townshend began his campaign to bring the colonies to heel. The Americans, he said, objected to "internal taxes," such as the Stamp Act, but would not oppose "external taxes," such as duties on imports. Therefore, he proposed and obtained the laws known as the Townshend Acts, which imposed duties on glass, paints, tea, paper, lead, and other materials imported from Britain by the colonies. Revenue raised by these taxes would be used primarily to pay the salaries of colonial governors and judges, who had heretofore been paid by the colonies and were thus obligated to them. Next, it would pay the expenses of British troops to be concentrated on the eastern seaboard. Finally, a Board of Customs Commissioners was to be established in America to make certain that these new taxes together with all other old taxes would be *collected*.

News of passage of the Townshend Acts did not immediately arouse the anger of the colonists. There was no sudden outcry, such as the clamor succeeding the Stamp Act. Instead, there was a growing uneasiness, which became a united protest only after John Dickinson of Pennsylvania explained why the acts should be resisted. Dickinson was a wealthy lawyer and gentleman farmer. He was also a student of constitutional law. His *Letters of a Farmer in Pennsylvania* were widely published in the American press, and in them he maintained that the Townshend duties violated the rights of Englishmen. He also observed that they were not really imposed to relieve the burden of taxation at home in England. The Townshend duties would raise at most £40,-000 a year. Compared to the estimated cost of government for 1767 of £8,500,000, this was a mere pittance.

In reality, argued Dickinson, the new laws were intended to assert the power of the crown over the colonies. They would pay in part for an unwanted and distrusted army and would make royal officials independent of the colonial assemblies which used to pay their salaries. Thus independent, the officials would be freer to defend British authority, and they would be backed up by British regulars present in the country.

These arguments, then, did much to convince Americans that the mother country was determined to treat them as stepdaughters. They also had no intention of paying the taxes, which they again sidestepped by smuggling. Meanwhile, the news that Charles Townshend, the author of their troubles, had died of a fever that summer did little to appease their resentment.

As practical as ever, the colonies reopened economic warfare. Boycotts of British goods were again enforced. Nonimportation agreements were made, and merchants who were reluctant to join them soon found themselves ostracized or even threatened with bodily harm. Violence was now common in America. At the encouragement of the educated, less educated men formed themselves into mobs, usually at the direction of agitators such as Samuel Adams. Muscular young Sons of Liberty roamed the streets to cow all who defended British authority. They fought openly with agents of the detested Board of Customs Commissioners.

Undaunted, the customs men continued to try to enforce the laws. In June, 1768, they seized John Hancock's sloop *Liberty*—probably on a charge of smuggling. At once, Boston was in an uproar. Angry crowds forced four customs commissioners to flee the city and to take refuge in Castle William, an island fort in Boston Harbor.

Now Britain was outraged. Troops were ordered into rebellious Boston. Down in New York City, Major General Thomas Gage, commander in chief of His Majesty's forces in America, felt confident that the mere presence of his redcoats would subdue Boston. Of Bostonians he said, "They are a people who have ever been bold in council, but never remarkable for feats in action."

But when two regiments of infantry arrived in Boston in October, 1768, they were greeted with cold hostility. Boston refused to quarter or supply them. Two more regiments landing later were similarly rebuffed. Without quarters, some units had to camp on Boston Common.

To the townsmen of Boston, the redcoats had come to crush their freedom, and they treated them with open contempt. Frequently, they taunted them as lobsterbacks, a derisive reference to the British Army's brutal practice of flogging wayward soldiers. Bewildered by contemptuous treatment from people who were, after all, British subjects like themselves, the regulars responded with hatred of their own.

Insult was returned with injury, and on March 5, 1770, the unavoidable conflict between the two forces occurred. On that date, a mob of Bostonians gathered before a British sentinel at the customshouse. The sentry called for help. A file of seven soldiers was sent to his rescue. Upon their appearance, the mob grew both in numbers and in boldness. Stones, snowballs, and taunts were hurled at the redcoats. Some of the Bostonians struck at the soldiers' muskets with clubs. One redcoat was knocked down. Someone, apparently a soldier, shouted "Fire!" One by one the exasperated regulars discharged their muskets. They killed five civilians and wounded six more, most of them innocent bystanders behind the mob. Now, the explosive incident known as the Boston Massacre had entered history.

Some of the dying had not yet sobbed their last before Boston was rallying to arms. Drums beat and bells rang to summon the militia. Musketmen poured into the streets. Two companies of them surrounded the Town House, and it is likely that rebellion might have erupted then and there had not Lieutenant Governor Thomas Hutchinson calmed the crowds by promising to bring the soldiers to trial. After all troops were withdrawn to Castle William, peace returned to Boston.

Tranquillity also returned to all the colonies after the eventual repeal of the Townshend Acts. Once again the boycott—not the belligerence of Boston—had had its effect in Parliament. With exports to America cut in half, the mother country decided to remove all but the tax on tea, and good feelings between London and the colonies were restored.

They lasted about two years. Even the boycott was forgotten, and the Englishmen living on the eastern seaboard of North America appeared to be among King George's happiest and most loyal subjects. Of course, the tax on tea still remained. But no one complained about it. That was because smugglers maintained a constant supply of Dutch tea, on which there was no tax. But then, on June 9, 1772, the British armed schooner *Gaspee* ran aground near Providence while chasing a colonial smuggler.

Like almost all seafaring colonials, Rhode Islanders had no love for customs officials. They especially disliked Lieutenant William Dudingston, skipper of the *Gaspee*, who had been arrogant to law-breaking and law-keeping sailors alike. That night, eight longboats full of angry colonials rowed out to the *Gaspee*, shot and wounded Dudingston, took him and his crew ashore, and burned his ship to the water.

Now it was Britain that was outraged. King George had been openly insulted. His officer had been shot, his men mishandled, and his ship burned. A royal proclamation was issued offering a reward for information leading to the arrest and conviction of the *Gaspee* culprits. A board was sent to Rhode Island to inquire into the incident. But there were no informers and no evidence. Instead, the Americans again turned resentful. What was a British board doing in the colonies? By what

26

right would they take a man from America to try him in England? Once more the colonials began to clamor against British invasion of their rights. Even though London discreetly dropped the inquiry, the outcry continued.

The Boston Massacre was remembered. Samuel Adams, long discontent because the boycott had been dropped, returned to prominence—and to anti-British propagandizing. Then, when Britain attempted to influence colonial courts by putting judges on the royal payroll, Massachusetts countered with a successful offer of higher pay. Next, Samuel Adams proposed the organization of Committees of Correspondence. These groups were to act as communication links between towns. They would tell one another what the British were doing and how they were being resisted. Other colonies set up their own committees. Thus, by 1773 a most valuable communications network was being formed in the colonies.

By that time a new political leader had emerged in Britain. He was Frederick, Lord North, who would guide the nation's fortunes for fifteen disastrous years. Tall, portly, popeyed and big-nosed, he bore a remarkable resemblance to King George. Like the king, he was personally a kind man, gentle and devoted both to his family and his Christian faith. In politics he was probably a good leader. However, he had two serious defects: He knew nothing about America or Americans, and he was extremely weak-willed. It was to Lord North, then, during that critical year of 1773, that King George turned in hopes of finding a solution to the problems of empire. And it was to North that the East India Company came, seeking a means of making the Americans buy its tea.

Of all the Townshend duties, of course, the tax on tea had survived. It remained because King George believed "there must always be one tax" to maintain the right to tax. But the ingenious colonists had simply evaded the tax by smuggling. Because of this, a huge backlog of 17,000,000 pounds of tea had accumulated in East India Company warehouses in Britain. The firm—in which the government had a deep interest—was faced with bankruptcy.

Lord North was concerned. He agreed that the government should repay the company for the duties it had paid to import the tea into England. Also, the company would be allowed to export its tea directly to its own warehouses in America; this would save money. Moreover, the East India Company would be allowed to pay a lower import tax in America, thereby making its tea cheaper to buy than the smuggled brands. In fact, the colonists would be getting their tea cheaper than it could be bought in England. Surely, Lord North reasoned, such an arrangement should satisfy even those proud and stubborn Americans.

Instead, it convulsed the colonies with anger again. Lord North had apparently not thought out the consequences. First, when the East India Company was allowed to export straight into its own warehouses, it cut out the American importer of tea. Next, by lowering the tax on tea, it offended the smugglers and dealers in smuggled tea. In those days, very few colonials considered smuggling immoral. Smugglers and dealers in smuggled goods were regarded as responsible citizens, and they very quickly joined forces with legitimate importers enraged by the "monopoly" granted to the company. In Philadelphia the merchants declared that anyone who abided by the Tea Act was "an Enemy to his Country."

Soon a campaign to prevent receipt of the tea was begun. American ship captains refused to carry East India tea. In Philadelphia and New York some ships actually took their cargoes of tea back to England. When three tea ships anchored in Boston Harbor, a group of "Mohawks"—actually Samuel Adams' Sons of Liberty disguised as Indians—boarded them, broke open the tea chests, and threw the contents over the side.

This was the Boston Tea Party. It infuriated King George, and he called upon Lord North to take action against Boston and the colony of Massachusetts. North's response was the four Coercive Acts. Under them, Boston was to be closed as a port, the Massachusetts legislature was to come under control of the crown, all the colony's officials were to be appointed by a royal governor, and town meetings—the soul of self-rule in New England—were to be held only once a year.

The North ministry did not obtain passage of these laws without opposition. Many famous Englishmen protested against them openly. They foresaw that, so far from bringing the colonies to obedience, they would actually drive them into open rebellion. But these voices were not heeded. The regulations which the indignant colonies were to brand as the Intolerable Acts were passed in Parliament. King George had lost all patience with his daughters across the sea. Now he was going to bring them into line.

3

"Americans" Are Born

The man whom King George named to enforce the Coercive Acts was Lieutenant General Thomas Gage. Already commander in chief of His Majesty's troops in America, Gage was also now governor of Massachusetts. He assumed this office in May, 1774, after he took up residence in Boston.

"Tommy" Gage was a typical British general. He was handsome, strong, brave, and dedicated. He was also, at least apparently, well qualified for his new position. He had had wide experience of America, having served with Edward Braddock and James Abercromby during the French and Indian War and having commanded the operations against Pontiac. Moreover, he was married to an American, the former Margaret Kemble of New Jersey.

Nevertheless, for all his American experience and all

31

his marital ties to Americans, General Gage had the same low opinions of the colonials as most Europeans of his time. He saw them as an irresponsible rabble who had to be chastised before they tore the British Empire apart. He despised them as soldiers. He had always regretted the repeal of the Stamp Act and most of the Townshend Acts. This was a fatal weakness, he believed, and it was one of which he would not be guilty. Lieutenant General Thomas Gage intended to enforce the Coercive Acts up to the very letter of the law.

Gage was not shaken by the cool reception he received in Boston. For weeks after his arrival, church bells had tolled dolefully, prayer and fasting had been proclaimed, and mourning badges had been displayed. Gage's reply to these suggestions that his arrival meant the death of liberty was to close the Port of Boston with a thoroughness that left the city paralyzed. His ships made certain that nothing went in or out of the harbor. One observer wrote:

"Did a lighter attempt to land hay from the islands, or a boat to bring in sand from the neighboring hills, or a scow to freight to it lumber or iron, or a float to land sheep, or a farmer to carry marketing over in the ferryboats, the argus-eyed fleet was ready to see it and prompt to capture or destroy it."

Meanwhile, the people of the city suffered. Without jobs, some sailors and workers left the city for the countryside. Most of Boston's 20,000 inhabitants stayed, however, their hearts and minds hardening against the "cruelty" of the mother country. When Gage sought information on the persons responsible for the Boston Tea Party, his investigators reaped a harvest of silence. His attempt to make Boston pay for the ruined tea met failure. When he thought to discredit John Hancock by depriving that vain patriot of his colonelcy of a company of cadets, the company retaliated by disbanding itself. And there were rumors that he had offered a bribe to Samuel Adams and been haughtily rejected.

Even the Massachusetts legislature which he convened in Salem proved defiant. First, the representatives quickly protested the removal of the provincial capital from Boston to that town. Next, they refused even to consider Gage's request that they compensate the East India Company for its lost tea. Finally, they began discussing a congress to make laws for all the colonies. Hearing of this, the alarmed Gage sent an order to dissolve the legislature. But the representatives locked the door against his emissary, while making their historic proposal for a Continental Congress.

Feeling against Britain was now running very high in Massachusetts. It was especially bitter in Boston, where the arrival of each new regiment of British redcoats caused resentment to mount. General Gage had once written, "They will be lions while we are lambs." Now he wrote: "We are threatened here with an open opposition by arms every day. . . ." Worse for the governor-general's peace of mind came news of passage of the Quebec Act.

Here was a law which sought to solve the problem of how to treat those new British subjects living in the province of Quebec who were mainly French and Catholic. To do so, it extended the province to include French settlements in the valley of the Ohio while recognizing French civil law and the Roman Catholic Church. As wise and humane a law as was ever passed in the reign of King George III, the Quebec Act nevertheless came at exactly the wrong time. If it pleased the French-Canadians, it inflamed the Americans. They saw it as merely another obstacle to westward expansion and support of a religion which they hated and feared. And the anger aroused by news of the Quebec Act had barely reached its reddest peak when Gage sent his soldiers out to seize stores of colonial powder and shot.

Marching into Charlestown and Cambridge, the regulars carried off colonial stores of ammunition—and with that mounted couriers went pounding over the lanes to spread the word of this latest British injustice. The next day, it seemed, the entire province was seething. Armed and angry farmers swarmed into Cambridge. From all over Massachusetts they came, singly or in town companies—fathers and sons, brothers, hunting companions —so that a citizen army as large as or even larger than Gage's force of about 4,000 men seemed to have sprung up on the plain.

General Gage was astonished. The spectacle of an army arising overnight was an entirely new experience to this veteran soldier. He did not, however, make any rash or hasty moves. Instead, the presence of the citizen army across the Charles River in Cambridge made it clear to him that Boston lay wide open to attack. So he put his men to work fortifying the city and closing off the narrow neck of land linking Boston to the mainland. In the meantime, hard on the heels of this confrontation, delegates from every town and district of Suffolk County —which included Boston—met at Dedham to pass the famous Suffolk Resolves.

Composed by Dr. Joseph Warren, an ardent patriot and the friend of Samuel Adams, the resolves bitterly assailed Britain as the enemy of freedom and declared that, if necessary, force must be used to defend liberty. They advised the province of Massachusetts to collect taxes on its own and to withhold them until the abhorred Coercive Acts were repealed.

These acts were denounced as "murderous law." Because of them, the streets of Boston were "thronged with military executioners." The Quebec Act was "dangerous to an extreme degree to the Protestant Religion and to the civil rights and liberties of all America. . . ." Finally, another boycott of British goods—complete and absolute—was recommended.

Not since the growing division between the mother country and her thirteen colonies had begun eleven years ago had there been a document as explosive as the Suffolk Resolves. The very savagery of its language betrayed the hurt and angry resentment of the people of the Boston area. So they were passed—and copied—and the riders went galloping over the lanes again.

One of them—a skilled silversmith named Paul Revere—turned his horse's head south for Philadelphia.

When the First Continental Congress assembled in Philadelphia on September 4, 1774, the delegates were about evenly divided between moderates and radicals. The moderates hoped to steer a cautious course, to make the mother country understand by respectful petitions and the like, while the radicals wanted direct action.

Eventually, these two factions were to become bitter rivals. They divided into patriots and loyalists, the first the fathers and fighters of the Revolution, the second remaining loyal to the mother country. Not all the moderates remained in the loyalist camp, of course. Many of them gradually were drawn to the patriot cause. But almost all the Loyalist leaders, such as the wealthy Joseph Galloway of Pennsylvania—men who would be attacked and abused as treacherous "Tories"—were originally moderates. They believed honestly and deeply that obedience to Britain was to be preferred to disorder, even if that meant a loss of liberty.

At the outset, the patriots led by John Adams of Massachusetts seized the initiative. They placed themselves in control of the Congress. Still, they did not press for an open break with Britain. Actually, few, if any, of the delegates were for a direct breach with the mother country. Even fiery patriots such as Samuel Adams or Patrick Henry and Richard Henry Lee of Virginia were in the minority. Most of the delegates were wealthy conservatives, such as Charles Carroll of Maryland or the Rutledges of South Carolina. Certainly George Washington, easily the most commanding presence at the Congress, both because of his height and his military reputation, preferred some kind of relationship. Not even John Adams would have gone along with his cousin Sam. "There is no man among us," he said, "that would not be happy to see accomodation [*sic*] with Britain."

But what was "accommodation" to be? What would make Britain relent: a soft word or a sharp protest? That was the question that divided the delegates—until Paul Revere came clop-clopping into town with his saddlebags stuffed with the Suffolk Resolves. At that moment, the radicals rallied. They read out the documents to a packed and hushed gathering. A vigorous debate began. In the end, the resolves were adopted by the Continental Congress itself. Now, all the colonies* were speaking with the same sharp tongue as the men of Suffolk.

"This was one of the happiest days of my life," wrote John Adams. "This day convinced me that America will support Massachusetts or perish with her."

Significantly, Adams had said "America." No longer, then, did the delegates think of themselves as Englishmen living on the eastern seaboard of North America. No. Now they were "Americans." And in that spirit, the Congress passed a declaration of rights and resolves. Audaciously referring to Great Britain as "a foreign power," the declaration served notice on Parliament that the people of America considered themselves bound

* The royal governor of Georgia had prevented that colony from electing delegates.

by none of its laws except purely commercial regulations. King George was respectfully notified that he still had his prerogatives, but that these must conform to strictly American ideas about the rights of men and their rulers.

No shots had been fired yet, but the American Revolution had begun.

4

Redcoats and Rabble

When the first shots in the American Revolution actually were fired, they were exchanged by forces which were apparently as evenly matched as a professional swordsman dueling a plowboy.

On the one side was the magnificent British war machine, which, chiefly because of its navy, was then the terror of the world. On the other, the Yankee militia, the so-called minutemen, a raw, undisciplined rabble in arms.

Although it would be the British navy's herculean task to support and supply a fighting force 3,000 miles away, the actual suppression of the rebellion was the duty of the ground forces: the British army. In 1775 the army consisted of fewer than 49,000 officers and men. This small but so-far effective force was stationed in British garrisons throughout the world. At no time would the crown ever be able to bring the full power of its land forces to bear against the Americans. In fact, the British army was never able to muster as many as 15,000 of its troops in America. Because of this, King George had eventually to call in mercenaries—that is, soldiers from other lands who fought for pay.

In this army, the basic fighting unit was the regiment. This was the largest body of troops which may be controlled within range of the commander's voice. Usually, a British regiment numbered 477 officers and men, although it could be as large as 1,000. In America, at the beginning of 1775, the nine regiments under General Gage were at about two-thirds of normal strength, so that they totaled about 4,000 men of all ranks.

To raise a regiment in those days, the British crown made a contract with some distinguished soldier or nobleman. To him as the colonel commanding the regiment, the crown paid so much for each soldier who enlisted. Thereafter, it paid him an annual sum to feed and clothe his men. Sometimes, instead of paying for the enlisted men, the crown would allow the colonel to select his own officers, to whom he would then sell a commission.

A commission certified a man's rank as an officer—that is, as a lieutenant or captain or major and so on up the line. When commissions were bought, they became the property of the buyer and could be resold upon his death or retirement. Thus, the system of purchased commissions restricted rank to men of means. Almost without exception, British officers were men of family, frequently the younger sons of noblemen. They did not go to military school because there were none in those days. Instead, they entered service at the age of sixteen or thereabouts and learned their profession of arms in the reality of war and military life.

The soldiers they commanded were often looked down upon as "the scum of the earth."* They were paid less than eightpence a day, and because they were charged for their clothing, medicine, and other necessities, they got practically no pay at all. Moreover, their food was wretched, the life was hard or boring by turns, and the discipline was brutal. It was not unusual for soldiers convicted of crime or disobedience to be sentenced to thousands of lashes. Sometimes their backs would be a bloody red pulp, and they would be near death before they were cut down. This practice disgusted the freedom-loving Yankees of America.

Obviously, few men would be willingly drawn to the low pay, bad food, hard life, and cruel discipline of the British army. So the judge and the bottle became the king's chief recruiters. Criminals were pardoned or debtors forgiven their debts if they enlisted in the army. Or else recruiters deliberately made strong young men drunk before they pressed "the king's shilling" into his limp hand. When a man took the king's shilling, of course, it was like taking the oath of enlistment. Occa-

---

* This is the phrase which the great Duke of Wellington unkindly used to describe his own soldiers, the conquerors of Napoleon.

41

sionally, foolish young boys would join, their heads turned by the beat of the drum or the glamor of the regular's scarlet coat.

Uniforms, of course, were another attraction. They were at the very least colorful, often gaudy. This was not so much to attract recruits as to distinguish different forces on the battlefield. They also made a stirring sight on parade. However, they were very impractical for active service. First, they were thick, stiff, hot, and tight. The British regular's scarlet coat was so lavishly decorated with colored linings, facings and pipings, brass buttons, and lace that it became extremely heavy. Beneath his coat, the soldier wore a waistcoat or vest of red or white. It was very tight, and so were his white breeches and his long buttoned gaiters, which often came to above his knee.

Stuffed into this gaudy straitjacket, strapped up in a bayonet belt around his waist and a cartridge belt from shoulder to waist, his head movements hampered by a stiff collar and a high, stiff leather collar under his chin, the British regular found it very uncomfortable to move. Worse, the hat the soldier wore had no brim or vizor to keep the sun out of his eyes. Finally, for ornamental purposes, the soldier had to wear his hair in a tight queue or ponytail, stiffened with grease and white powder, with tight curls in front of his ears.

Just to keep himself clean and neat required two or three hours a day of a soldier's time. He had to pipe-clay his leather—that is, whiten it—black his shoes, clean his cloth, polish his buttons, braid and dress his hair, and, finally, keep his bayonet and musket in gleaming, shining order.

The musket with its affixed bayonet, of course, was the basic weapon of the British army. There were other arms or branches of the service such as engineers, artillery, and cavalry, but the foot troops or infantry armed with the musket and bayonet were the fundamental fighting arm. Massed in a regiment's subdivisions of companies and battalions, they were taught how to wheel left or right, to march forward or backward, to form oblique at a sharp angle to the enemy's front—in short, to be at least as responsive to their commander's shouted orders as his horse would be to the pressure of his hand.

This was the style of battle of the day. Armies confronted each other on battlefields, often open plains. With drums beating and sometimes with bands playing, they marched and countermarched. But all these feints and pretended attacks or retreats which seemed to occupy so much of the army's time in silly, if colorful, "maneuvers" had a definite objective. They were intended to deceive the enemy on when and where the real blow would fall.

When this blow did come, it was usually at one of three points of the enemy's line. These points are the two flanks, or the ends of his formation, and his center. The object was to turn or envelop the enemy's flank— that is, to get around either his right or left end and get into his rear. Or else a commander struck at his opponent's center in an effort to break through his line and thus disorganize his troops.

In all these movements, the decisive maneuver was a charge by the infantry. Sometimes the cavalry would be involved, but usually it was the infantry that won or lost the battle. In the end, then, the warfare of the late 1700's depended primarily on the discipline and drill of the foot soldier and his skill with musket and bayonet.

In Britain the musket was the famous Brown Bess, named for Queen Elizabeth. It was a 10-pound muzzle-loader. To load it, a British soldier took a paper cartridge from the leather box strapped to his side. This cartridge contained both powder and a lead ball three-quarters inch in diameter. Biting the cartridge open, the soldier sprinkled a little powder on the pan of his piece. Then, placing the musket butt-downward, he poured the rest of the powder down the barrel. Next, he pushed in the ball. Crumpling the paper into a wad, he crammed that in afterward. Finally, seizing his rifle rod, he rammed all—powder, ball, and paper—down tight inside the barrel.

To fire the musket, he placed the butt against his shoulder and pulled the trigger. This released a cock which struck its flint against a piece of steel to send a shower of sparks into the pan. When the powder here ignited, it flashed through a touchhole into the bottom of the barrel and exploded the charge which propelled the bullet down the barrel.

When a ball from a Brown Bess struck a human

being, it could cause a grievous wound, if only because it was much larger than the bullets of today. However, the musket had a very short killing range, and the ball would fall harmlessly to the ground after 125 yards. Moreover, the musket was not very accurate, and the British soldier was a poor marksman. Actually, he did not "aim" his musket but merely "pointed" it at the enemy. The British manual of arms did not even include the command "Aim!" And because the rate of fire was a slow two or three shots a minute and the musket often misfired (being useless in the rain), the Brown Bess was not the fearful weapon that history sometimes says it was. In battle the British redcoat depended more on the bayonet, a slender, pointed 21-inch length of steel attached to the muzzle of his musket.

Usually, the musket was hardly more than a noise-and-smoke-making machine. The British line would advance to within a hundred yards of the enemy, when one or more hit-and-miss volleys would be fired. Then, bursting out of the smoke raised by their discharge, yelling wildly, the regulars would charge with the bayonet.

This was the tactic which the Americans dreaded most. Just because they were normally a poorly disciplined crowd of ill-armed and ill-trained citizen-soldiers, the colonial militia did not have enough moral stamina to stand firm in the face of a bayonet charge.

Militia, of course, were not regular soldiers enlisted for long periods of time and compelled to live a life in uniform like the troops of the armies of Europe. Militia was not a force in being, like a standing army. Instead, it was

45

a force in potential, one which would be brought together in an emergency. Thus, in Massachusetts, every able man between sixteen and sixty was required to possess a firearm and to be enrolled in his township's company.

These men would elect their own officers and "meet" for drill about four times a year. Usually, a meeting was as much a social as a military event. The companies would gather on the village green under the eyes of their relatives and sweethearts, who had probably packed a lunch for the occasion. Laughing and joking with their officers, who were, after all, their neighbors, the militiamen would go through maneuvers and mock skirmishes in an easy, careless style that appeared comical to the trained military men of England. Sometimes, they would break formation to gather around the girls and tease them, firing off their muskets to frighten them and then bursting into guffaws at their screams. This was the figure of a Yankee militiaman that so amused an English gentleman that he immortalized it in the words of the song "Yankee Doodle."

Few of these troops were uniformed. Rather, they wore homespun, dyed in the brown juices of the local tree barks. Their guns were a hodgepodge of calibers and vintages. Some militiamen had Brown Bess muskets issued during the French and Indian War. Others had older pieces dating as far back as Queen Anne's War (1702–13). Among these "modern" weapons were mingled old firelocks and fowling pieces, blunderbusses and horse pistols—anything that would fire ball or buckshot. Rifles—those highly accurate new weapons designed by immigrant German gunsmiths for the backwoodsmen of Pennsylvania and Virginia—were unknown in Massachusetts.

For ammunition, the militiaman carried a powder horn and bullet pouch—or cartridge box—together with a bullet mold for making his own ball and an extra supply of flints. In the field, he would also have a haversack and blanket roll. Some militiamen, but not many, had bayonets.

This, then, was the amateur force which the professional arms of Britain were making ready to crush. By the end of 1774, however, Massachusetts had taken steps to improve the quality of its military. Appropriating the huge sum of £15,627 to purchase military supplies, the Provincial Congress also called for the organization of minutemen. This meant that one-third of its militia was to be alerted to act "on a minute's notice." The Congress also named three generals to command the militia and set up a Committee of Public Safety under Dr. Joseph Warren.

Everywhere in Massachusetts, now, militiamen were drilling on the green. All the laughter and the pranks and the gay carelessness had disappeared. Instead, deadly serious "Yankee Doodles" had begun to surprise British outposts to steal their powder and guns. British forts were raided, and as colonial supplies began to increase, General Gage sent out expeditions to seize them. In one foray into Salem on February 26, 1775, a force of regulars and militia under Colonel Timothy Pickering met at a bridge. The British commander ordered Pickering to withdraw, but he stood his ground. War might have come right then and there, had not a clergyman persuaded Pickering to allow the redcoats to make a token march of thirty rods into town, where, discovering nothing, they turned and marched back to barracks.

To Patrick Henry in Virginia, however, hostilities seemed to have commenced already. Arising in the House of Burgesses, he cried: "It is in vain, sir, to extenuate the matter. Gentlemen may cry, 'Peace! Peace!' —but there is no peace. The war is actually begun! The next gale that sweeps down from the north will bring to our ears the clash of resounding arms! Our brethren are already in the field! Why stand we here idle? What is it that gentlemen wish? What would they have? Is life so dear, or peace so sweet, as to be purchased at the price of chains and slavery? Forbid it, Almighty God! I know not what course others may take; but as for me, give me liberty or give me death!"

In England the choice had already been made. The Fisheries Act, the last of the repressive measures aimed at bringing the Americans to heel, had been passed. New Englanders were forbidden to trade with the mother country and prohibited from the Newfoundland fisheries. Massachusetts replied by reviving the Provincial Congress and putting itself on a virtual war footing. On April 14, General Gage in Boston received his "get-tough" orders. Force was to be used to crush the rebellion, and the ringleaders were to be arrested.

The fight for liberty was now truly to be to the death.

5

The Shot Heard Round the World

General Gage had been kept intimately informed of the patriots' moves by a traitor among them. The informer was Dr. Benjamin Church, the well-bred and charming grandson of a famous old Indian fighter of the same name. Because of his family's standing and his own attractive qualities, Dr. Church had been appointed to the Committee of Public Safety.

He told General Gage that the committee had been secretly gathering an arsenal at Concord. He also informed the general of the whereabouts of the patriot ringleaders. Dr. Warren was somewhere in Boston, Sam Adams and John Hancock were in Concord, and John Adams was even farther out in the country.

Determined to carry out his orders to crush the rebellion with all possible speed, General Gage decided to send a force out to Concord with instructions to seize the rebel arsenal and capture Sam Adams and Hancock. The troops he chose for the mission were his best: the light infantry and the grenadier guards companies. These were known as the flank companies. Because of their fighting skill and bravery, they went into battle on the posts of honor at either flank. Between 600 and 800 of these elite redcoats were alerted to move out quietly on the night of April 18.

During daylight of that date, General Gage dispatched mounted officers to scout the road to Concord and to capture patriot couriers. Unknown to him, of course, the couriers were already on their own alert and waiting for dark to move.

Dr. Warren had his own spies. He knew that the flank companies had been taken "off all duties till further orders" and he did not believe that this was merely to learn "new evolutions," as Gage had ordered. Patrolmen such as Paul Revere and William Dawes had seen the transports in Boston Harbor hauling up their whaleboats for repairs, and they guessed correctly that a troop movement by water from Boston to Cambridge and thence by land to Concord was likely.

Alarmed, Dr. Warren ordered Revere to ride out to Concord to warn John Hancock and Sam Adams. Riding back that night, Revere arranged "that if the British went out by water we would show two lanterns in the North Church steeple; and if by land, one." This signal, the famous "one if by land, two if by sea" in Longfel-

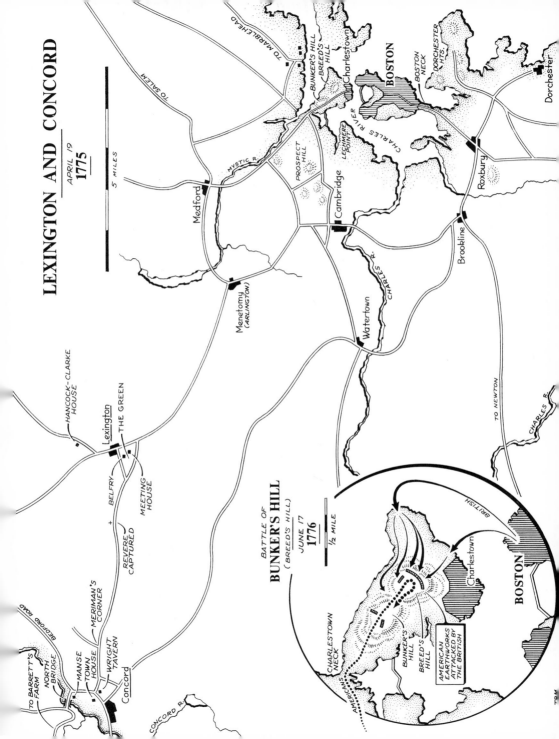

LEXINGTON AND CONCORD

APRIL 19
1775

5 MILES

TO MARBLEHEAD

TO SALEM

BUNKER'S HILL
BREED'S HILL
Charlestown
BOSTON
BOSTON NECK
DORCHESTER HTS.
Dorchester
Roxbury
Brookline
TO NEWTON
CHARLES R.

MYSTIC R.

PROSPECT HILL

LECHMERE POINT

CHARLES RIVER

Medford

Cambridge

Watertown

Menotomy
(ARLINGTON)

HANCOCK-CLARKE HOUSE

Lexington
THE GREEN

BELFRY

MEETING HOUSE

REVERE CAPTURED

MERIMAN'S CORNER

WRIGHT TAVERN

TOWN HOUSE

MANSE

NORTH BRIDGE

TO BARRETT'S FARM

BEDFORD ROAD

Concord

CONCORD R.

BATTLE OF
BUNKER'S HILL
(BREED'S HILL)

JUNE 17
1776

½ MILE

CHARLESTOWN NECK

BUNKER'S HILL
BREED'S HILL

Charlestown

BOSTON

AMERICANS

BRITISH

AMERICAN EARTHWORKS ATTACKED BY THE BRITISH

low's poem, was intended to arouse the townspeople across the harbor in the Charlestown area, while Revere and his co-courier Dawes galloped out into the Lexington-Concord countryside.

On the night of the eighteenth, General Gage's picked troops filled their packs for a full day's march and went to bed early. About ten, they were awakened by their sergeants. Whispering to one another, feeling their way by hand, they dressed and slipped out of their barracks —leaving their sleeping comrades behind. Then, as though to mock all this elaborate secrecy, they formed ranks and marched openly to Boston Common. There they were met by their commander, Lieutenant Colonel Francis Smith, a fat, slow man. Colonel Smith's second-in-command was Major John Pitcairn of the Royal Marines, one of the finest field officers in the British armed forces. At about half past ten, in full view of observers on the common, the regulars began marching down to the waiting whaleboats.

Long before the silent boatloads of regulars shoved off onto the dark waters of Boston Harbor, William Dawes and Paul Revere were out arousing the patriot countryside. Dawes took the longer land route, galloping over Boston Neck to Cambridge and from there to Menotomy (now Arlington) and the road to Lexington and Concord. Paul Revere, meanwhile, had himself rowed to Charlestown. Booted and wrapped in a greatcoat to keep out the raw April chill, he sprang onto his horse and went clattering into history.

"The regulars are out!" Revere cried, shouting at every lighted window he passed. Coming upon darkened homes, he dismounted to throw handfuls of gravel at the windows. The moment a candle or lantern flickered into light, he cupped his hands to his mouth to shout, "The regulars are out!" Mounting his horse again, he galloped off into the night.

At Lexington, Revere rode straight for the home of Parson Jonas Clark, where Clark's cousin John Hancock was staying with Samuel Adams. There, the guard told him to stop making so much noise.

"Noise!" Revere snorted. "You'll have noise enough before long. The regulars are coming out."

At once, the guard awakened Adams and Hancock. Dressing, they fled across a meadow, where Adams paused to exclaim: "What a glorious morning this is!" It was then about midnight, and when Hancock appeared puzzled by the reference to daylight, Adams added: "I mean for America."

Meanwhile, William Dawes had also ridden into Lexington, where he joined Paul Revere. Setting out for Concord, the two couriers met young Dr. Samuel Prescott, who came with them to help warn the countryside. Halfway to Concord, the trio rode straight into the arms of Gage's mounted scouts. All three tried to escape. Dawes turned and rode safely back to Lexington. Dr. Prescott jumped a stone fence and galloped onward to

Concord, where he warned the militia. But Paul Revere, riding a tired mount, was cornered in a pasture and taken captive.

Nevertheless, the countryside had been warned.

Long before dawn lighted the Lexington-Concord road, Colonel Francis Smith realized that there would be no surprise that day. Instead, it seemed, there would be trouble. For one thing, his redcoated regulars were very unhappy. The whaleboats had "landed" them in knee-deep water at Lechmere Point, after which Colonel Smith had "led" them straight into a waist-high backwater of the Charles River. Drenched, each man weighed down by about sixty pounds of equipment, the soldiers finally gained the road. And there the ringing of alarm bells and the crackling of warning shots made it plain that the patriots knew of their coming. Marching into Menotomy at about half past three in the morning, Colonel Smith was informed by outriders that the rebels had been alerted. Alarmed, he sent a mounted courier back to Boston with a request for reinforcements. Then he ordered Major Pitcairn ahead to Lexington with the advance guard, while he followed with the main body.

Lexington Green was set within a triangle formed by three roads. There Captain Jonas Parker had formed his company of about seventy men. They stood about a hundred yards above the Lexington-Concord road, which formed the base of the triangle. Daylight of April 19 had come, and as Parker and his men stood there, they saw the approach of Major Pitcairn and the British advance guard.

The redcoats came closer. Sunlight danced on the burnished barrels of their Brown Bess muskets. It made points of light on the tips of their gleaming bayonets. Some of Captain Parker's men shifted uneasily. One man said, "There are so few of us, it is folly to stand here."

"The first man who offers to run shall be shot down," Parker said.

Silently, fearsomely, the regulars came on. Then Pitcairn gave an order, and they formed line of battle. Cheering and shouting, the rear ranks of redcoats surged forward on the double, and the entire force deployed in two sections three men deep. On Lexington Green, some members of the ragged patriot band fidgeted.

"Stand your ground!" Parker commanded. "Don't fire unless fired upon. But if they want to have a war, let it begin here!" Hearing those brave words, a few of Parker's men shook their heads and left the green. The rest stood firm.

Riding forward, Major Pitcairn shouted, "Lay down your arms, you damned rebels, and disperse!"

Now Captain Jonas Parker saw that his situation was impossible. He could not hope to halt the British. Still, he would not obey Pitcairn's order to surrender his weapons. Telling his men to disband, Parker also ordered them to keep their firearms. Again and again Pitcairn demanded that the departing patriots lay down their arms. Suddenly, shots crashed out. They could have been fired from the British ranks on the road below or from some patriots behind a wall. To this day, it is not known who fired first. But a British soldier was wounded and Pitcairn's horse was twice grazed by musket balls.

Angered, a British officer bellowed, "Fire, by God, fire!" A volley of musketry crashed from the road into the green. Americans fell. Captain Parker was wounded. Alarmed, anxious to stop the bloodshed, Major Pitcairn spurred his horse forward. "Soldiers!" he cried. "Soldiers, don't fire! Keep your ranks. Form and surround them." But the redcoats paid their commander no heed. Their blood was up. These were the very same Yankees who had taunted and tormented them for months. Now let them sneer at the "lobsterbacks." Reloading, they lifted their muskets once more. Desperate, Pitcairn unsheathed his sword and swung it downward in the signal to cease fire. In reply, the regulars discharged another volley.

For a moment, it appeared that the Yankee farmers in homespun might give battle. Some of them fired in return. But the American volley was ragged and harmless. Exultant, the redcoats cheered and charged with the bayonet, and with that the militia fled.

Only Jonas Parker stood his ground. Though stricken, he had been one of those who fired at the British. Even with the redcoats charging, he stood firm to reload his musket—and British bayonets cut him to the ground.

The Battle of Lexington—a tiny skirmish big with history—was over. Eight Americans lay dead on the green. Ten more had been wounded. Only one British soldier had been harmed. But blood had been spilled by both sides. Major Pitcairn was aware of the consequences when he gravely re-formed his jubilant men. So was Colonel Smith when he arrived later with the main body. Now, the British knew, marching west to Concord, they had a war on their hands.

Most of the patriot arms which the British hoped to seize had been stored at the farm of Colonel James Barrett, several miles northwest of Concord. Much of this had been sent even farther west the day before. But Barrett's home still contained many muskets and light cannon, together with bags of powder and barrels of ball. And so, minutes after young Dr. Prescott galloped into town with the word that the regulars were out, Colonel Barrett and a force of militiamen went hastening over North Bridge to Barrett's farm.

Arriving there, some militiamen carried the barrels of ball into the attic and covered them with feathers, while others hauled the powder bags into the woods, and a plowman dug furrows in which the muskets and cannon were laid and covered with earth. Satisfied, Colonel Barrett and his men returned to North Bridge, where they joined hundreds of other minutemen brought into Concord by the ringing of the alarm bell. Now Barrett had about 400 men under his command. He kept them on a ridge overlooking North Bridge from his side of the Concord River. From this height they could see the redcoats marching into town.

While Colonel Smith and his staff went to a tavern for breakfast, four companies of light infantry crossed North Bridge under the eyes of Barrett's men. No shots were fired while this force of about 160 soldiers went up the road to Barrett's farm. Behind them another group of about 120 redcoats guarded North Bridge on both sides of the river. This was to be sure to keep the bridge open for the other unit's safe return.

Meanwhile, back in Concord itself, British grenadiers began to search the town. Polite but firm, they moved from house to house, finding about 100 barrels of flour and 100 pounds of bullets, which they threw into a mill-pond. Gun carriages discovered in the Town House were set afire and then put out when it was feared that they might set the building on fire. So they were dragged outside, where they were relighted.

Smoke from the fire was seen by Barrett's men on the ridge across North Bridge. "Will you let them burn the town down?" an angry officer asked Barrett, and the colonel ordered his militia to march to the rescue. Led by Captain Isaac Davis, marching in a column of twos to the measured beat of the drum strapped to the frail body of little Abner Hosmer, they came down the ridge and approached the bridge.

Surprised, Captain Laurie of the British outpost there sent back into town for reinforcements. Two companies of grenadiers were formed, but because they were led by the slow-moving Colonel Smith, they were not in time. In the meantime, the alarmed Captain Laurie pulled his cross-river outposts back to the Concord side of the bridge and re-formed there. Still, to his astonishment, the Yankee militia came on. They meant to fight, he could see, and he gave the order to fire.

Once again on that momentous "19th of April, Seventy-five," British ball crashed out toward Americans. The first shots fell short. The British front rank soldiers turned and ran to the rear to reload while the second rank presented their muskets and discharged them. This time they found the range. Captain Isaac Davis was killed, and little Abner Hosmer fell dead beside him. Two other Americans were wounded. Now the British second rank had retired to reload, making way for a third volley from the third rank.

"Fire, fellow soldiers!" an American officer pleaded. "For God's sake, fire!"

They did. At last, an aimed and disciplined American volley tore into the redcoated ranks of Britain. Three soldiers fell dead, and nine more were wounded. Stunned, the redcoats broke ranks and rushed back to town. The Americans cheered and ran after them. But the pursuit was only for a few yards. The demoralized British light infantry had rushed full tilt into the ranks of Colonel Smith's rescue force of grenadiers and could be observed re-forming. At that point, it was possible that the patriots might be caught in a trap. In front of them was Colonel Smith's force re-forming on the road from Concord. Somewhere across North Bridge behind them were the four companies of light infantry which had marched out to Barrett's farm. Should they appear suddenly in the patriot rear, the militiamen might be caught between two fires. And this, perhaps, could have persuaded the triumphant Americans to give up the pursuit.

Instead, they returned to the bridge to recover the bodies of Captain Davis and drummer boy Hosmer. Then they went back to the ridge. On the road by the deserted bridge lay the bodies of three dead redcoats and one wounded man. Suddenly, a farmer carrying an ax came onto the bridge. In horror he saw the soldiers sprawled there. The wounded man stirred. Frightened, the farmer struck at him with his ax and ran away.

At Barrett's farm, meanwhile, the light infantry had found nothing. Disappointed, they began marching back to Concord. It was now almost ten o'clock in the morning, and they had been on their feet since ten o'clock the previous night. They were tired. Their thick stiff uniforms had dried on their bodies, and now they were rumpled and hot. Reaching North Bridge, the light infantry wheeled right, crossed—and came upon the bodies of their fellow redcoats. They saw the "scalped" soldier, and their step quickened. They began to run. To the delighted amazement of the watching Yankees on the ridge, the British light infantry—pride of the army —went tearing into Concord in terror.

There, they were given a two-hour rest by a grave-faced Colonel Smith. He had accomplished neither of his missions—failing either to seize the patriot arms or to capture their leaders—and now he must make a sixteen-mile return march through what could very well be a hostile and armed countryside. At noon, hoping that the reinforcements he had requested were on the way—he gave the order to move out.

General Gage had indeed sent reinforcements out to Colonel Smith. In fact, he had anticipated the need and ordered a full brigade of troops to parade at four o'clock that morning. However, in the way of all armies, the order was not received—and Colonel Smith's appeal for help did not arrive until five o'clock that morning. Then it was sent to the wrong place, so that it was not until nine o'clock in the morning that a full brigade of about 1,000 regulars and marines, with two cannon, struck out across Boston Neck.

They were commanded by Brigadier General Hugh Earl Percy. At Lord Percy's order, his fifes and drums began to play, and just to show his contempt for the ragged rabble he was marching out to chastise, the band played "Yankee Doodle."

Colonel Smith and his redcoats had begun to respect "Yankee Doodle." Their return march to Boston had been turned into a retreat, a running of a bloody gauntlet. All along that sixteeen-mile route, the Yankees had been gathering. They came from towns and villages too far from either Lexington or Concord to have joined the skirmishes there. Nevertheless, they arrived in time to take up their positions on either side of the road. From Concord to Boston, perhaps as many as 4,000 Americans entered the battle.

They all did not fight at one time. Some stayed just

long enough to fire a few balls at the redcoats before returning home. Others might keep abreast of the British for a half dozen miles, harassing them with musket fire from behind stone fences or trees, sometimes dashing up to within a few yards of the road to blaze away at the enemy. Others maintained a running fight the entire length of the way.

Eventually, as the galling fire from both sides of the road began to take a bloody toll, the redcoats fought back. Colonel Smith sent parties of light infantry out to his flanks to strike at the Yankees. They set up ambushes, surprising the militia and shooting them down. Occasionally, they cornered bands of patriots in roadside houses and bayoneted them to death, after which they set the houses afire.

Still, the banging of guns from either side of the road continued. Redcoats continued to fall. The carriages which Colonel Smith had hired in Concord were piled high with wounded. Even British discipline was shredded by that relentless, horizontal hail of lead. Smith's neat columns eventually became a disorderly crowd of frantic men. Soldiers broke ranks to ransack roadside houses for food or whatever they could carry off. The disorganization became so dangerous that Smith halted outside Lexington and ordered Pitcairn to hold off the Americans while he re-formed his ranks.

At that point, the patriots attacked Pitcairn's rear guard. Marksmen behind a pile of rails took aim at Pitcairn and struck his horse. Plunging, the beast threw his rider and galloped into American lines, carrying off the marine major's set of horse pistols. But the British held, and Smith re-formed his men. They marched into Lexington—stumbled, rather, for they had been on their feet for twenty hours. The combination of fatigue and terror—the twin scourges of war—was whittling their will to continue. They were on the verge of breaking into a rout, when they saw Lord Percy's relief force drawn up in a fighting square. Too tired to cheer in jubilation, they marched inside the square "their tongues hanging from their mouths, like those of dogs after a chase." Meanwhile, Percy's cannon kept the patriots at a respectful distance.

Some time after three o'clock, with Percy now in command, the retreat was resumed. Once again, the patriots hung on the British flanks like bulldogs. Worse, they had received reinforcements and a semblance of organization. General William Heath and Dr. Joseph Warren had come out to Lexington to try to organize the American attack. But their efforts were futile. The Yankee musketmen preferred to fight Indian style rather than form into companies which might have set up roadblocks across the British line of march. Here the Americans displayed that lack of military skill which was to weaken the patriot cause throughout the early years of the war. Nevertheless, they kept striking the enemy flank. And Percy's fresh troops fought back. They drove the rebels into roadside houses and bayoneted them there. Halting again and again, Percy unlimbered his little cannon to drive off the Americans. Finally, they entered Charlestown and could see the masts of the British warships in the harbor. A few more leagues, and they were under the protecting guns of the fleet.

The retreat was over. The battles of Lexington and Concord had been fought. The British had lost 73 killed and 26 missing—probably dead—and 174 wounded, a total of 273 casualties out of about 1,800 men engaged. The patriot losses were 49 killed, 5 missing and 41 wounded, a total of 93.

There would be bigger and bloodier battles during the eight years of agony and ordeal that lay ahead. But there would be none larger in significance. The "shots heard round the world" had been fired.

6

A Gentleman from Virginia

The skirmishes at Lexington and Concord had powerful effects on both sides of the conflict that was to be known as the War of the American Revolution.

Among the colonies, reports of these "victorious battles," as the skillful patriot propagandists described what was at best a standoff in two minor clashes, resulted in a growing pride in American military prowess. It also caused the colonies to harden their attitude toward the mother country. Convinced that Lexington-Concord had been a British attack on American liberty, they clamored for more outright action.

Up and down the coast, militia companies were drilling openly. There was a rapid increase in the manufacture of powder and ball, and the daily wearing of uniforms became popular in both village and city.

Such sights naturally brought thousands of Americans who had been wavering between the two sides crowding into the patriot camp. Tories who had been hoping for an end to the Boston revolt sadly packed up their belongings and departed for the sanctuary of either Canada or England itself.

The royal governors of the colonies also rushed for the protection of British arms. With almost all the British regulars cooped up with Gage in Boston, they were powerless to put down rebellion in their own provinces. They were also left to the mercy of patriot militiamen who would have liked nothing better than to tar and feather them. As a result, they either ran away or took safety aboard British warships. Only Lord Dunmore of Virginia attempted to enforce British law, and he was quickly ousted from Williamsburg by a force of patriot militia led by Patrick Henry.

Into this explosive atmosphere then, amid a rising clamor for common action against a common foe, came Lord North's latest "peace proposal." Having had second thoughts about the wisdom of using force in America, the king's first minister had devised a new "peace plan." It offered freedom from taxation to any colony which volunteered to pay a fair share of the cost of empire. In effect, Lord North was saying, "If you give me the money of your own free will, I will not make you give it to me." Here was peace at pistol-point, a proposal which was to be backed up by reinforcements which his lordship had been collecting for America.

However, when it arrived in America on the day after

66

Lexington-Concord, it was treated as though it were beneath contempt. Even General Gage had not much faith in it. He had seen at first hand how little the colonials were to be influenced by peaceful overtures. He had also seen, on the day the ship carrying the proposal sailed into Boston Harbor, that the colonials had cut him off from the mainland.

Almost the moment that Lord Percy's exhausted regulars had been rowed across the harbor to the sanctuary of the city, abandoning vital Charlestown Neck, thousands of armed patriots had come swarming into the area. Forming into an army under the command of General Artemas Ward, these raw mechanics and farmers were set to work throwing up fortifications and building an armed camp to seal off the city from the countryside.

Within a matter of days, General Gage found himself completely cut off. For both supply and reinforcements, he would now have to depend on the sea behind him. By then, of course, the British commander in chief had lost his contempt for the Americans. He no longer despised them as an ignorant rabble in arms. Rather, he shared Lord Percy's newfound respect for the Yankees, expressed in the remark "Whoever looks upon them as an irregular mob will find himself much mistaken." Gage now believed that a force of no less than 32,000 regulars would be required to crush the revolt, and a stream of pessimistic letters from himself to his superiors in London began to explain why he felt his mission would be so difficult.

First, the countryside was unmistakably hostile. British dreams of an America actually more loyalist than patriot, of what might be called a huge "fifth column" eagerly awaiting the chance to rally to the king, were a delusion. True, at no time during the Revolution was America ever much more than half patriot and half loyalist, but the fact was that the patriots had the Tories completely terrified and demoralized. Social ostracism, threats of force (even the use of force), tarring and feathering, loss of business—these were a few of the tactics which the rebels used to make the Tory fidelity to the crown a very timid allegiance indeed. Worse, America was then a country of between 2,500,000 and 3,000,-000 people.

From this, the patriots could draw upon a pool of about 450,000 males of military age. Granting even that many of these would be Negro slaves or loyalists or people unwilling to fight for a variety of different reasons, this was still a very respectable reservoir of manpower. With the Yankees thus close to a source of troops, and Gage 3,000 miles away from his own source, the problem of a supply line was that much more difficult.

Food supply was another pressing problem. Once again, the countryside was hostile. The rebels had cut Gage off. By June the British were on very lean rations. One officer wrote: "However we block up the port, the rebels certainly block up our town, and have cut off our good beef and mutton." Because it was impossible to ship live cattle from England, the British would have to raid the rebel coasts to acquire fresh meat. As Gage knew, this would not be easy, and so salted beef and pork would have to be shipped from home. In fact, all the foodstuffs that Gage required—not only meat but oats for the horses, butter, peas, oatmeal, flour, and so on—had to come 3,000 miles across the sea. Every year in America, one-third of a ton of food was required to feed each man, besides the weight of the casks in which it was shipped. Between men and food and other gear such as camping, cooking, and ordnance equipment, General Gage faced an enormous problem in what is called logistics—the supply, movement, and quartering of troops. Every year the war in America was to require tens of thousands of tons of supply, all of which had to cross the sea in the small, slow, frail sailing ships of the day. All this would be exposed to loss from bad quality, imperfect loading and shipping, theft, and deterioration owing to storage or climate. There would be other losses through delay, storms at sea, or the attacks of American privateers. Thus, the cost of carrying on the war in America would easily outstrip the Seven Years' War just ended, and the supply problem would be so immense that it would not be equaled until the total wars of the twentieth century.

Finally, the very character of America and the Americans promised to make this costliest of British wars also the longest. The extreme cold of the northern colonies would rule out winter campaigning there, and the burning heat of the southern summers would restrict operations in that season. Any movement more than a few dozen miles into the wilderness of the American interior would also be difficult. Also, road networks were poor, and the existing highways were hardly more than wagon ruts. The very ruggedness of the American countryside, interlaced as it was with broad rivers, made battle in the accepted European style almost out of the question. Thus, the terrain in which the war was to be fought would be far more suitable to the American tactics of Indian fighting and the American strategy of delay. Obviously, to General Gage a prolonged war would be more to the advantage of the rebels than the crown. And even though British sea power might make it possible for General Gage to strike anywhere along the colonial coast, there was no single capital city the capture of which might end the war. In those days, the fall of a capital such as Paris or London or Madrid usually meant the defeat of the nation. In America, however, there was as yet no United States with a single capital city. Instead, there were still thirteen different republics, each with a capital of its own.

These, then, were the serious difficulties which confronted General Gage, and he wrote constantly about them to London. In fact, he may have been too frank. Certainly Lord North had begun to lose confidence in him. So had the British cabinet. Only the king's reluctance to disgrace this veteran soldier had saved him from prompt recall. Instead, when reinforcements were collected to help load the "pistol" behind North's "peace plan," it was decided to send three major generals to Gage's assistance.

They were Sir William Howe, Sir Henry Clinton, and Sir John Burgoyne. Here was the famous "triumvirate of reputation," a trio of generals with records so awe-inspiring that Lord North is supposed to have said, "I do not know whether our generals will frighten the Americans, but they certainly frighten me."

Of the three, Sir William Howe was considered the ablest. He was a fine tactician—that is to say he was skilled in the movements which win battles. Tactics, of course, are the means by which battles are fought. Like a boxer, a tactician probes for his enemy's weakness and then, finding it, attacks it. Sir William was most adept in this branch of the military art. At Quebec under Wolfe, it was he who had led the "forlorn hope" up the secret cliffside path to the Plains of Abraham, thus penetrating the "impenetrable" French defense. Howe had also been selected to train the light infantry, to instruct them in the lessons learned in the irregular warfare against the French and Indians. Also, he came of exceptionally "good family" and was said to be related to the king himself. Like King George, he had a heavy face and large bulging eyes. Like his older brother, Admiral Lord Richard "Black Dick" Howe, he was of dark complexion —and he had no enthusiasm for the war.

The Howes were Whigs, members of a political party which opposed the powerful Tory Party's attempt to solve the American problem by force. More, they were sympathetic to the Americans, who had placed in Westminster Abbey a statue of their brother, Lord George Augustus Howe, the much-esteemed commander who had been killed at Fort Ticonderoga in 1758. With many other Whig officers of the army and navy, the

Howes had said they would not serve against the colonies. They agreed only upon the king's request, and in the case of Sir William, at least, because of a need for the rewards in money and rank which would come from such service.

Sir Henry Clinton, the next experienced general, was a less colorful career soldier. The son of an admiral and former governor of New York, he had been in uniform since the age of thirteen, when he purchased a lieutenant's commission. At twenty he was a lieutenant colonel, and at thirty-four a major general. An able planner of military operations, General Clinton was also an inward-looking, sensitive man. He resented criticism and was extremely jealous of his reputation.

In contrast, the third member of the generals, "Gentleman Johnny" Burgoyne seemed not to have a care in the world. Man-about-town, playwright, wit, Burgoyne appeared more at home in salons and gambling houses than on the fields of war. Yet he had served with distinction in Portugal during the Seven Years' War and was known to be one of the progressive generals who believed in treating soldiers more like humans than dogs. However, like most gentlemen with large tastes and small fortunes, he was not above intriguing for promotion and pay. He was on the king's payroll to vote in Parliament as the king wished him to vote, and the flattery which he poured into the royal ear was helpful in getting him aboard the frigate *Cerberus*, bound for fame and fortune in the war against the colonies.

On May 25 the *Cerberus* arrived in Boston Harbor,

and the three generals conferred with General Gage. Not having requested the "triumvirate of reputation," Gage was not especially happy to see them. He was annoyed to receive orders to pay each of them £500 for military equipment. Gage had served in America for twenty years, and he had never received as much as twopence for such expense. Miffed, General Gage promptly put in a request for £500 of his own. Also, the commander in chief did not share London's faith in the "triumvirate's" power to frighten the Yankees. He would have preferred 3,000 men to the three generals— especially now that the patriots had captured Fort Ticonderoga.

At dawn of May 10, 1775, Ethan Allen assembled about 80 of his "Green Mountain Boys" outside Fort Ticonderoga. In the murky half-light, Allen's huge figure seemed to dwarf the smaller, stocky figure of Benedict Arnold standing beside him. Arnold had come to Ticonderoga as the military agent of Massachusetts, but Allen, armed with orders from the Connecticut Assembly, had got there before him. And it was Allen who was in command.

"I now propose," the big Vermonter said, "to advance before you and in person to conduct you through the wicket-gage. For we must this morning quit our pretensions to valor, or possess ourselves of this fortress in a few minutes. Inasmuch as it is a desperate attempt—which none but the bravest of men dare undertake—I do not urge it on any contrary to his will." He paused and then, raising his voice, cried, "You that will undertake, poise your firelocks!"

To a man, the Green Mountain Boys lifted their muskets. Forming three ranks deep, they followed the tall Allen and the shorter Arnold toward the stone walls of the fort. A sentry saw them approach, pointed his piece, and pulled the trigger. But it misfired, and the soldier ran back inside the fort shouting the alarm.

"No quarter! No quarter!" the Americans cried, chasing him. Within the fort, a second sentry struck at an American with his bayonet, slightly wounding him. Allen slashed him across the face with his saber and pounded up the staircase with Arnold close behind him. At the head of the stairs stood Lieutenant Jocelyn Feltham, assistant commander of the fort. He was struggling to put his breeches on.

"Come out of there, you damned old rat!" Allen bellowed, and the stunned Feltham asked him by what authority he had entered the king's fort.

Waving his sword menacingly, Allen shouted, "In the name of the Great Jehovah and the Continental Congress!" With that, the frightened officer summoned Captain William Delaplace, who at once surrendered his command of forty men and Fort Ticonderoga.

The Americans had swung open the gate to Canada.

News of the seizure of Ticonderoga shook the Second Continental Congress. To all the delegates assembled in Philadelphia, it was plain that this event, even more

74

than Lexington-Concord, meant that there was no turning back. Here it was the colonials, not the British, who had been the aggressors. And here it was a royal fort that had fallen. The king himself, not just the "ministerial troops," as the patriots called the British soldiery, had been attacked.

Grave as the situation now appeared, the delegates were nevertheless heartened to hear that the Americans had again done well in combat. Colonel George Washington, in charge of a committee to supply the colonies with munitions, was pleased to learn that "Ti" had yielded about sixty cannon and mortars. If these field pieces could be moved, they could be put to good use outside Boston.

Meanwhile, Congress began to consider an appeal from Massachusetts to adopt the army outside Boston as its own.

The request was a clever one, for if all the colonies assumed control of the army, naming generals to command it, as well as providing recruits for it, that would mean that all the colonies would be solidly behind Massachusetts against the mother country. The delegates, of course, saw what the consequences of such a measure would be—and some of them drew back. However, John Adams, now the spokesman for all New England, was determined to unite the colonies behind his native province. He arose in Congress to make it clear that all the colonies shared a common danger. If the New England colonies were abandoned to their fate, then Britain, having chastised them, would turn to punish all the others. To prevent this, he said, there must be an "American" army supported by all the colonies.

The next question was: Who would command it? General Artemas Ward now commanding outside Boston was forty-eight years old and confined to a sickbed. Who would take his place? Strangely enough, there were not too many candidates—or at least not many men with any real professional experience. All but a few of the commanders who had fought the French and the Indians were dead or too far gone in years. There was, of course, Charles Henry Lee, a former British officer who was a general by the grace of the King of Poland. Lee was well known for his military skill and his passionate espousal of the cause of liberty. Major Horatio Gates was another former British officer who had taken up residence in America. However, it seemed that it would be wiser to choose a native-born American.

John Hancock, then serving as President of the Congress, had military ambitions—as John Adams well knew. But Hancock's experience was limited to the parade ground. Besides, it seemed that election of a Southern man would do most to unite the colonies. And so the short, rotund Adams fastened his eyes on the figure of the tall, slender gentleman from Virginia— George Washington. Appearing daily in his old uniform, Washington had impressed most of the other delegates with his grave, calm demeanor and his military bearing. Thus, on June 14, when Adams nominated him for the command, his name was quickly approved by the Congress.

Informed of his appointment as "Commander-in-Chief of the forces raised and to be raised in defense of American liberty," Washington arose with characteristic modesty to say, "I declare with the utmost sincerity, I do not think myself equal to the command I am honored with. As to pay, Sir, I beg leave to assure the Congress that as no pecuniary consideration could have tempted me to have accepted this arduous employment at the expense of my domestic ease and happiness, I do not wish to make any profit from it."

Thus, he would keep an account of his expenses, and that would be all the pay he would expect.

Satisfied, Congress next moved to name Washington's lieutenants. Artemas Ward, of course, was continued in his rank of major general, which was also conferred on Charles Lee; on the wealthy Philip Schuyler of New York; on Israel Putnam, to keep Connecticut happy; and, finally, as a professional adjutant to do Washington's staff work, on his neighboring Virginia planter, Horatio Gates.

As quickly as he could detach himself, George Washington left Philadelphia to take charge of his army. Before he could reach Boston, however, it was back in combat again.

7

The Whites of Their Eyes

When the British retreated from Concord into Boston, they abandoned Charlestown Peninsula. Eager to be free of the Yankee army buzzing about their ears, they had crossed the bay into the sanctuary of the city and thus left this vital isthmus open to seizure by their enemy.

This was unwise. Who controlled Charlestown Peninsula commanded Boston. Artillery emplaced on Bunker's Hill or on the lesser height of Breed's Hill to its front could shoot across the bay into Boston and pound the city into submission.

General Gage, of course, was aware of this, as were the three generals who had joined him. They had even drawn up plans to occupy Charlestown, which lay due north of the city, as well as Dorchester Peninsula, directly south. However, news of the operation leaked out, probably because General Burgoyne talked too much, and the alarmed Committee of Safety called a council of war to consider seizing Bunker's Hill before the British could move.

By then, mid-June, 1775, there were as many as 15,-000 men in the patriot camp. Even so, General Ward and Dr. Warren were reluctant to move. First, the "army" was hardly more than a homespun mob armed with a motley of muskets and knives. Second, the two commanders feared that the British fleet might easily bombard them on the exposed height, while landing a force at their rear to cut them off. Moreover, there were only eleven barrels of powder in the patriot camp.

Major General Israel Putnam thought differently. "The Americans are not at all afraid of their heads," he told the council, "though very much afraid of their legs. If you cover these, they will fight forever." "Old Put" was listened to with respect. At fifty-seven, this muscular, vigorous, valorous soldier was a living legend. He had been with Lord Augustus Howe when he met death at Ticonderoga, had barely missed being burned at the stake by Indians, had been captured by the French, and had been shipwrecked while leading an expedition to Havana. His courageous words and his confident manner moved the council to act swiftly, and on the night of June 16 "Old Put" led about 1,200 Americans out on Charlestown Peninsula.

Putnam rode a fine horse, his saddle holsters stuffed with Major Pitcairn's lost pistols. Beside him was Colonel William Prescott, a soldier of very limited battle experience, but for all that a brave and practical man. When the force came to Bunker's Hill, Prescott wanted to stop there—as ordered—and entrench. The daring Putnam, however, rashly insisted that they take a more exposed position farther east on Breed's Hill. Although this height was closer to the British, it was also farther away from the American camp. So it was decided to place the main works forward on Breed's Hill, while fortifying Bunker's Hill to its rear to cover any possible retreat.

In the darkness, Colonel Richard Gridley, the force engineer, marked out the lines of the position. This was an earthen redoubt roughly 40 yards square. Conscious of the militiamen's well-known fondness for protection, he designed a 6-foot parapet above firing platforms of earth and wood. At the redoubt's northeast or left-front corner he also outlined a 6-foot breastwork 100 yards long. In all, the fortification was an extensive one, and at midnight, Colonel Prescott, fearful that he would not have time to construct it, ordered his men to begin digging.

Here, of course, the Yankees were at their best. Throughout the war the British would marvel at the speed with which the Americans could entrench themselves. Always, it seemed, they were better with spades than with muskets, and on this fateful night they dug with a willing fury.

Came dawn, and lookouts on the British warships in the harbor rubbed their eyes to see the earthen fort that had been thrown up while they slept. Almost at once, the warships opened fire. But their cannonade fell short and did little more than frighten the patriots, who had never heard such a roar.

The British, meanwhile, were holding their own council of war. Gage and his three generals agreed that the rebels must be attacked and ousted from the peninsula. But how? General Clinton suggested that the fleet land a force to the rebels' rear. This was a good plan, but it was not adopted. Instead, General Gage ordered Howe to cross the harbor and advance along the northern shore of the peninsula. This would "outflank" the rebel redoubt—that is, get past it and threaten the American rear, thus forcing them to abandon the position. Although the order was issued in the morning, the harbor tide was running against the British. Six vital hours were lost before Howe could begin landing his troops.

The delay granted the Americans valuable time in which to finish the redoubt on Breed's Hill. Still not satisfied, Colonel Prescott cast his anxious eye to his left —the very point at which Howe proposed to strike—and saw that it was wide open. Calling again on his spademen, he ordered them to extend the fortification in that direction. They began to dig again, and as they did, cannonballs fell among them. One tore off the head of carefree young Asa Pollard. At once Prescott leaped up on the redoubt parapet to calm his horrified troops. And the breastwork to the left was finished.

To the rear, at Bunker's Hill, Israel Putnam rode back and forth across shot-swept Charlestown Neck to ask for reinforcements. Refusing at first, General Ward relented and sent Colonel John Stark and his New Hampshire regiment of sharpshooters marching to the rescue. Although they had come to camp with little ammunition, they were issued flints, powder, and lead cut from the organs of a Cambridge church.

They reached Bunker's Hill just as the British began to land on the peninsula.

Of the 2,300 men at his command, General Howe took about 1,500 across the harbor, leaving the remainder in reserve. Coming ashore at about one o'clock, the British commander saw at once that he could not turn the American left so easily. The enemy had extended his line there. Studying Bunker's Hill to the rear of Breed's Hill, he saw troop movement and fancied that this covering force was a sizable reserve. Next, seeing Stark's regiment of sharpshooters marching from Bunker's to Breed's, he concluded that the Americans were strengthening their defenses—and decided to call for reinforcements of his own.

In that second delay, the Americans again improved their position. The practical Prescott filled out his left by sending Connecticut troops and two cannon to a stone-and-rail fence that ran down to the Mystic River bank, after which Colonel Stark stationed a force of marksmen behind a barricade on the beach below. Taking the remainder of his sharpshooters, Stark posted them behind the fence where the Connecticut troops and their two cannon were stationed.

The American left was now firmly anchored on the river. Prescott's position was formidable. It consisted of the redoubt, the fence, and the beach barricade. Holding it were about 1,400 men, including Dr. Joseph Warren, the chairman of the Committee of Safety and now a major general. Grasping a musket, resplendent in a pale-blue waistcoat laced with silver and white satin breeches, Dr. Warren had come out to Breed's Hill from Cambridge. Seeing him, Prescott at once saluted and offered him the command. Warren graciously declined. "I shall take no command here," he said. "I came as a volunteer with my musket to serve under you." With that, he mounted the firing platform beside Prescott's militiamen.

By then Howe's reinforcements had arrived. The British general now had about 2,500 men opposing 1,400 on Breed's Hill. Dividing them evenly, he placed half under Brigadier General Sir Robert Pigot, who held down the British left and was to take the redoubt, while taking personal command of the other half on the right. This force was drawn up opposite the Yankee breastwork, fence, and beach barricade.

"I expect you to behave like Englishmen and as becometh good soldiers," Howe told his troops. "I shall not desire any of you to go a step farther than where I go myself at your head."

Before either of the British wings could move, however, Pigot's troops on the left began to suffer from the fire of Yankee snipers shooting from the houses in Charlestown. At once Pigot notified Admiral Samuel Graves, commander of the fleet, who ordered his ships to set the town afire.

Showers of red-hot cannonball and carcasses—that is, perforated iron balls filled with pitch—began falling on the town. Land batteries on Copp's Hill in Boston joined the bombardment, and soon Charlestown was blazing—houses, churches, shipyard, shops, and all.

Now Howe was ready to attack. He ordered an artillery barrage to cover the advance of his troops—that is, to keep the Americans down so that they could not fire on his charging men. Eight British cannon and howitzers began firing. Almost as quickly, to Howe's immense annoyance, they stopped. Someone had mistakenly supplied these 6-pound field pieces with mostly 12-pound balls, too big to fit their muzzles. When Howe requested grapeshot—clusters of musket balls, much like a charge of large buckshot—he was told that the artillery had sunk into the marshy ground at the foot of Breed's Hill. They were too far away to fire grape effectively. So the British assault had to go forward without artillery support.

Opposite the redoubt, little General Pigot's men began climbing the hill. Before they were in range, some nervous Americans opened fire. Angered, Prescott swore he would kill the next man who pulled the trigger. Meanwhile, a young officer ran along the parapet kicking up leveled muskets. On came the British.

Opposite the breastwork and fence, Howe's main

body formed and stepped out. Behind the breastwork, Israel Putnam rode back and forth to shout encouragement, bellowing the famous words "Don't fire until you see the whites of their eyes! Then fire low."

Opposite the beach barricade, Howe formed 350 picked light infantrymen in columns of four. They were to storm the position, led by the elite Welsh Fusiliers. Suddenly, Colonel Stark ran out from the barricade. Forty yards out, he drove a stake into the ground. Returning to the barricade, he shouted, "Not a man is to fire until the first regular crosses the stake."

Now, everywhere, the regulars were advancing. They marched with a slow, steady, terrifying pace. Against the breastwork and fence, however, thick grass impeded the attack, and a brick kiln and adjacent ponds fragmented the red ranks. Nevertheless, they came on—with General Howe hoping that the assaults both there and against the redoubt would distract the Americans so that his bayonet charge on the beach wall would carry through.

Beginning to run, bayonets outthrust, the Welsh Fusiliers raced past Colonel Stark's stake—and the Yankee muskets spoke. The redcoat lines were torn apart. Whole groups lay sprawled on the ground, still, kicking, or crawling away. Into the breach came the King's Own Regiment, hoping to close with the bayonet before a second volley was discharged. But Stark's sharpshooters fired again, and the red lines crumpled once more. Now it was up to the flank troops of the Tenth Regiment. Forming, charging, confident that no third volley could be prepared in such short time, they swept forward. And the third volley did crash out, and that was the end of the light infantry charge.

A stunned and disbelieving Sir William Howe mounted more assaults, leading them all with the personal courage which was one of his great virtues. But the Americans behind the fence and the barricade were invincible. Again and again their deadly fire riddled the oncoming regulars. No fewer than ninety-six soldiers perished, with many more wounded. To Howe's left, the assault on the redoubt was also repulsed. Mortified and white-faced, the British general called off the assault, while he requested more reinforcements and gave his men a rest. In his own words, this first experience with entrenched Americans had given Sir William Howe *"a moment that I never felt before."*

Although the Americans were jubilant, their commander was not so elated. True, his men had stopped the finest troops in the world, but Colonel Prescott knew that desertions had whittled the redoubt defenses to 150 men. Calling upon Putnam for reinforcements, he received only a reluctant few—just as the British attacked a second time.

Once again Howe was depending upon a direct frontal assault to overwhelm the "amateur" Yankees, and once again he chose to ignore the fact that his men would be exposed to volley after volley before they could reach the enemy fortifications.

That was what happened. On the left, Pigot was

forced to retreat, after the brave Major Pitcairn died leading a charge of marines. On the right, Howe's main body was shattered once more—and the entire attack was called off. Nevertheless, it had produced a telling toll among the Americans. It was not that any men behind the fortifications had been killed or wounded, but that the rate of desertions had grown. Every time a man was actually wounded there were as many as a dozen others "volunteering" to carry him—and themselves— to safety. Perhaps worse, the patriots had shot off most of their ammunition. There was enough ball, but very little powder. Cannon cartridges were broken open to supply this deficiency, but even this was not enough.

Below Breed's Hill, meanwhile, the British had received both reinforcements and more guns. Sir Henry Clinton had crossed the harbor at the head of 400 more soldiers and marines. He joined Pigot for the assault on the redoubt, while Howe deployed against the breast-work. While British cannon began firing, a demonstra-tion—that is, a feint to keep the Americans in place— was made opposite the beach barricade. With this, the red lines surged forward for the third time.

"As soon as the rebels perceived this," Lord Francis Rawdon wrote later, "they rose up and poured in so heavy a fire upon us that the oldest officers say they never saw a sharper action. They kept up this fire till we were within ten yards of them. They even knocked down my captain, close beside me, after we had got into the ditch of their entrenchment."

Once inside the ditch, however, the maddened redcoats were unstoppable. They scented victory and the chance to avenge their lost comrades, and they poured over the parapet into the redoubt. Little General Pigot, unable to vault the wall, climbed a tree outside the fort and swung himself into it. From three sides, now, the British came. The American fire ceased. Some Americans, notably Prescott and Dr. Warren, fought on with bayonets, swords, or clubbed muskets.

"Twitch their guns away!" Prescott shouted. "Use your guns for clubs."

It was too late, British bayonets were flashing and dripping red. More and more redcoats came springing over the walls. "Give way, men!" Prescott cried. "Save yourselves!" For himself, Prescott fought on—until he was finally borne outside the back gate on a tide of fleeing Americans. As he left, he passed Dr. Warren, directing the retreat. And then the brave doctor also fell—his blue waistcoat and fine white breeches smeared with mud and blood.

Now the British gave pursuit, and Prescott joined Israel Putnam in conducting a running retreat. Moving from fence to fence, they were able to delay the redcoats long enough for most of the Americans to flee Charlestown Peninsula for the safety of Cambridge. Nevertheless, it was in the retreat that the Americans suffered most of their casualties.

All told, the patriots lost about 150 men killed and another 300 wounded. British losses were 226 dead and 828 wounded, for a total of 1,054 against the American total of 450. True enough, the clash which history mistakenly records as the Battle of Bunker's Hill was a British "triumph." They had routed the rebels and regained the peninsula. But they won at an enormous loss of reputation.

8

Campaign in Canada

On July 3, 1775, sixteen days after the Battle of Bunker's Hill, General George Washington took command of the force outside Boston that now was to be known as the Continental Army. Washington had been impressed by reports of the recent action against British regulars, and he had been pleased to find his army was "very healthy." This, however, was about all that satisfied the new commander in chief.

First, the army itself was too small, only 14,500 men— hardly more than half of what Washington would have liked. Next, there was a dearth of trained engineers, a shortage of artillery, no war chest, and only enough powder to issue each man nine cartridges in the event of a British attack. The "camp" itself, if it could be so called, horrified Washington. Only the Rhode Island troops had arrived equipped with tents. All the others dwelt in huts or lean-tos scattered over a sprawling, smoking, stinking encampment in which every man cooked his own mess and the intermingling of sleeping quarters, latrines (or necessary houses, as they were called), and food-rationing centers made for a huge unsanitary mess. One visitor to the camp, the Reverend William Emerson, grandfather of Ralph Waldo Emerson, left this account of what he saw

Some [huts] are made of boards, some of sailcloth, and some partly of one and partly of ye other. Others are made of stone and turf, and others again of birch and other brush. Some are thrown up in a hurry and look as though they could not help it—mere necessity—others are curiously wrought with doors and windows done with wreathes and withes in ye manner of a basket.

To the Reverend Mr. Emerson, this checkerboard of shacks and shanties seemed "rather a beauty than a blemish in the army." To George Washington, it was a blemish, and he promptly began cleaning up the camp and restoring order and discipline. Company messes were set up. Old latrines were filled in and new ones dug on the outer edges of the dwelling area. Unsanitary piles of rotting meat and bones which had drawn swarms of disease-bearing flies were burned and buried. Where he could, Washington regularized the living quarters, hoping to achieve that uniformity which would give his ragged army a semblance of discipline.

Discipline, of course, was the chief problem. The

carefree Yankee with his democratic habits did not take easily to the rigor and regulation of military life. Most of the officers had been elected, and the ordinary soldier did not leap to obey orders from a man whom he had just helped to raise from the ranks. Often, a man's popularity, rather than his ability to command, had most to do with his acquiring rank. In this democratic army, it was not unusual to find a lieutenant shaving a private or a captain mending a corporal's musket. Washington hoped to put an end to this, and he began by cracking down on unworthy officers. As he wrote himself:

I have made a pretty good slam among such kind of officers as the Massachusetts government abound in . . . having broke one Colonel and two Captains for cowardly behavior in the action on Bunker Hill—two Captains for drawing more provisions and pay than they had men in their company—and one for being absent from his post when the enemy appeared there and burnt a house just by it. Besides these, I have at this time one Colonel, one Major, one Captain and two Subalterns under arrest for trial.

The new commanding general was also hard on the men in ranks, and he regularly ordered the flogging of drunken soldiers. Flogging, of course, was common in the armies of the day, and although Washington was humane enough to reject the crueler punishments which were equally common, he did have frequent recourse to the whip. Once he asked Congress to increase the number of permissible lashes from the Biblical limit of 39 to 500, but Congress refused.

92

Washington also attempted to provide some sort of uniform for his homespun-clad soldiers, at one point requesting Congress to provide him with 10,000 hunting shirts. Congress, however, decided upon a different uniform of brown cloth with facings in the regimental colors. Eventually, this was rejected, and eleven of the thirteen colonies chose dark blue as the uniform color, usually with facings of buff. Thus, blue and buff became the accepted colors of the Continental Army.

Keeping this army in being was easily George Washington's most vexing problem, the one with which he had to struggle throughout eight long years of war. The chief difficulty was short-term enlistments. Moderns, accustomed to long-term enlistments of up to four years or else, during total war, "for the duration of the emergency," find it hard to understand that the democratic soldiers of the 1700's agreed to serve for periods as brief as three months. In Washington's new army, most of the enlistments were due to expire on January 1, 1776—some men claimed it was December 1, 1775—and most of the soldiers refused to reenlist. In other words, the very army that Washington was then trying to mold into an instrument of battle would melt away in his hands by the end of the year. Equally trying, the various states were raising militia of their own and often offered higher bounties than the Continental Army could afford. Finally, some of the colonies, such as distant Georgia and South Carolina, were reluctant to supply him with men.

Nevertheless, Washington persevered. Gradually, he

evolved a true military organization. It was based on regiments of the line. Each regiment consisted of 720 men and officers formed by eight 90-man companies, in each of which there was 1 captain, 2 lieutenants, 1 ensign, 4 sergeants, 4 corporals, 2 "Drums and Fifes," and 76 privates. It was for these new regiments that Washington did most of his recruiting, and in so doing he also enlisted black men.

At that time, there were about 600,000 black people, almost all of them slaves, living in America. Most of them dwelled in the South. When the war began, the British tried to encourage them to revolt against their masters by offering them their freedom. Lord Dunmore employed blacks in his unsuccessful attempt to impose discipline on Virginia. Most of the Southern colonies, however, feared to put weapons in the hands of their slaves. Other slaveholders, especially in the Northern and Middle states, were only too eager to send black men to the colors as substitutes for themselves. The North also contained quite a few free blacks, some of whom had joined the New England army. One of them, Salem Poor, fought with distinction at Bunker Hill. Crispus Attucks, a black slave, was one of the martyrs shot down in the Boston Massacre.

Washington's problem was what to do with these black men. Congress had decreed that none of them should be reenlisted for the Continental Army. But then Washington reported that if he did not take them, they would become embittered and perhaps join "the Ministerial Army" opposing him in Boston. So Congress agreed to allow Washington to enlist black soldiers, so long as they were all freedmen.

Meanwhile, the new commander in chief was also occupied in gathering a staff of competent officers around him. One of his first finds in Boston was Henry Knox. This fat, amiable, and able artillerist had kept a bookstore in Boston and had read and learned so much about ordnance that his knowledge amazed even those British professional artillery officers who came into his shop. Another capable New Englander was Nathanael Greene of Rhode Island. Greene was a Quaker who had been read out of meeting because he had gone to war in violation of Quakerism's doctrinal belief in pacifism. A handsome man who walked with a limp and suffered from asthma, Greene was a bold, enterprising, and ingenious commander. Bold also, and brilliant as well, was Alexander Hamilton of New York. Eventually this young captain of artillery became one of Washington's most trusted aides.

Major General Charles Lee had also come to camp. Lean, hawk-nosed, slovenly, accompanied by a pack of yapping dogs wherever he went, this quarrelsome, if competent, general would always give Washington as much pain as pleasure. He was undoubtedly a capable and widely experienced officer. In his youth he had served in a regiment commanded by his father, later distinguishing himself in Portugal and receiving honorary appointment as a major general from the King of Poland. However, General Lee secretly resented Washington as an "amateur," and although he did not openly

95

criticize his chief, he could not refrain from impressing everyone he met with his own superior "expertise." With the resignation of Major General Artemas Ward, Charles Lee became the second-ranking officer in the Continental Army.

Of all these men it is doubtful if any were as capable in combat as Benedict Arnold of Connecticut. Certainly no one was more audacious or intelligent or masterful in action. Arnold seemed to thrive on adversity, the high quality of all born combat leaders. The greed and ambition which eventually were to lead him into treachery had not yet fully possessed Benedict Arnold, and so it was that when Washington decided to send an expedition into Canada, he gave the command of that force to the bold man from Connecticut.

At first, Congress had sought to make Canada co-partner in the rebellion. As early as the fall of 1774 the First Continental Congress invited the French-Canadians of the province of Quebec to choose delegates to the Second Continental Congress. They did not reply, chiefly because the royal governor, General Sir Guy Carleton, prevented circulation of the patriot appeal and because the Roman Catholic Bishop of Quebec and the local aristocracy were satisfied with British rule. Unable to coax Canada to their side, the Americans decided to conquer it.

Congress was aware that there were only four regiments of British regulars in the entire province and that these were strung out from Quebec City to distant outposts on the Great Lakes. With Gage cooped up in Boston, Canada seemed wide open. Unfortunately, Congress did not take immediate advantage of its northern neighbor's weakness. If, in May, when Ticonderoga fell to Ethan Allen, the Americans had quickly poured through this gateway into Canada, they probably would have made an easy conquest. But Congress was still uncertain about taking the offensive against Britain, until the Battle of Bunker's Hill changed its mind. On June 27, a full five weeks after the fall of Ticonderoga had opened the gateway to Canada, Congress finally authorized Major General Philip Schuyler to take command at the fort and to invade Quebec if he thought he would be successful.

Even here, Congress did not order a direct attack, and in leaving the decision up to General Schuyler, it almost guaranteed that there would be none. Schuyler was not a man of action. He was a wealthy aristocrat more able in conference than in combat. Once at Ticonderoga, he lingered there for many weeks. His excuse was that he needed time to collect men and supplies. Actually, he preferred to assume a defensive posture at Fort Ti. In the meantime, General Sir Guy Carleton was busy strengthening Canada's defenses. He put a strong force in Fort St. Johns on the Richelieu River.

Fortunately for the colonies, Schuyler's second-in-command was Brigadier General Richard Montgomery. Another former British officer who had settled in America, Montgomery was experienced and bold. Chafing at his senior's delays, on August 28 he took advantage of

Schuyler's absence in Albany and embarked on Lake Champlain at the head of 1,200 men. Schuyler soon joined him. The expedition sailed down the Richelieu River, only to be blocked by the British garrison at Fort St. Johns there. Schuyler became ill and returned to Ticonderoga.

Montgomery was left in charge. He now had about 2,000 patriots at his command. Among them was Ethan Allen, who had joined Montgomery as an individual volunteer, and a fighting lawyer named John Brown. Opposing the Americans were about 700 British—three-quarters of them regulars—under Major Charles Preston. Moving rapidly, Montgomery quickly surrounded the fort. Now, it seemed, Canada was in real danger. The largest single force of redcoats in the province was besieged in Fort St. Johns. Should they surrender quickly, the way to Montreal would be clear.

The British did not give in so easily, however. Week after week went by as Montgomery tried to storm St. Johns or bombard it into submission. But the British held out stubbornly. Still, Montgomery kept them under siege. Meanwhile, he sent parties under Ethan Allen and John Brown to the north to clear the advance to Montreal and to recruit Canadians for the patriot cause. When Allen and Brown met in the enemy rear, they decided to attack Montreal on their own. Brown with 200 men would strike above the town, and Allen with 100 would hit it below. When the time came, however, Brown did not appear. Undaunted, Allen attacked on his own—and was routed and taken prisoner.

The loss of Allen did not discourage Montgomery. Resolved to take St. Johns before winter, he floated gun batteries past the fort to force the surrender of Fort Chambly downriver. Now cut off from Montreal, Preston was compelled to surrender, and on November 2, 1775, he hauled down his flag. Without hesitation, Montgomery moved against Montreal. Warned of his approach, Carleton stripped the city of its troops and moved downriver to make a last stand at Quebec. On November 12, Montreal fell to Montgomery.

A few days later the American commander prepared to join Benedict Arnold at Quebec.

Benedict Arnold had been among the first to propose an invasion of Canada. He had gone to Philadelphia to lay his scheme before Congress and had been frustrated to see his general plan adopted and the command given to General Schuyler rather than himself. Still nursing his resentment, Arnold had gone to Boston, arriving just as Washington began to consider mounting his own expedition against Quebec. Washington believed that Carleton would be too busy defending Montreal to have time for Quebec City. A quick, daring strike, he reasoned, should wrest this ancient fortress from Britain's grasp. And who better to command it than Arnold?

Offering Arnold a colonel's rank—which the ambitious man from Connecticut eagerly accepted—Washington placed about 1,000 men under his command. Most of them were Yankee militiamen bored with the life in the Boston camp, but there were also three companies of Pennsylvania and Virginia riflemen. These sharpshooters, together with their fellow backwoodsmen from Maryland, had arrived in Boston armed with the famous Kentucky rifle. This was the long, slender weapon which Swiss and German gunsmiths living in Pennsylvania had designed for the American frontier. Musketmen, firing their clumsy inaccurate ball, rarely could hit a man at 60 yards, but the riflemen could put shot after shot into a 7-inch target at ranges up to 250 yards. At first Washington welcomed the arrival of these marksmen, until his guardhouses began to fill up with them. The expedition to Canada, it seemed, would be just the adventure for these rambunctious spirits. So they "jined up," led by old Captain Daniel Morgan, a born leader who had arrived in camp still bearing the scars of the flogging he had received under Braddock at the Monongahela. Nineteen-year-old Aaron Burr was another recruit.

At the head of these men, Arnold planned to ascend the Kennebec River in Maine and descend the Chaudière to the St. Lawrence, taking Quebec by surprise while Carleton was busy with Montreal. In late September, several weeks after Montgomery began the siege of Fort St. Johns, they began their march. Almost immediately, Arnold's dream of a rapid stroke turned into a nightmare march.

The advance was through a wilderness. The 200 bateaux, or flat-bottomed boats, which had been made for the expedition were too heavy to drag over the numerous portages between waterways. And there were many more portages than the maps had shown. Some of the bateaux came apart. Others sank, with men and provisions aboard. Eventually, the boats had to be abandoned. Then the food gave out. Men ate soap and hair grease. They boiled or roasted their moccasins and bullet pouches and ate them. They devoured their dogs. Blundering through woods, sloshing through swamps and fords, some men became lost. Others died. So great became the ordeal that about 350 men turned back. At last, on November 9, forty-five days after they had set out on their "three-week march," Arnold and some 600 scarecrows stumbled out of snow-cloaked forests onto the south bank of the St. Lawrence.

With characteristic speed, Arnold at once began collecting boats to cross the river. Strong winds, however, thwarted him, and it was not until the night of November 13 that he began to cross. On the following morning, he stood with his ragged little army on the Plains of Abraham. It was here that James Wolfe had defeated the Marquis de Montcalm to win all Canada for Britain. Here, sixteen years later, Benedict Arnold hoped to win Quebec for the colonies.

But he had arrived too late. Before he could cross the St. Lawrence, Lieutenant Colonel Allen Maclean had entered Quebec at the head of about 100 Scots soldiers. This gave Quebec a total of 1,200 defenders and, more than that, the skill and energy of Maclean to direct the defense. Realizing that he could not storm the citadel alone, Arnold retreated about twenty miles upriver to await the arrival of General Montgomery with reinforcements. In the meantime, Sir Guy Carleton, traveling in disguise, slipped into the city and began to build its troop strength to about 1,800 men and to strengthen its fortifications.

It was not until December 2 that Montgomery joined Arnold. He brought with him 300 men, as well as artillery, ammunition, and food and clothing for Arnold's starved and shivering soldiers. With his little army well rested and fed, it would seem that General Montgomery —now in overall command—was ready to besiege Quebec in the same way that he had reduced Fort St. Johns.

Unfortunately, a harsh winter was closing in, the ground was too hard to dig approaches—that is, siege trenches—to the city walls, smallpox had broken out in his own camp, and his artillery had been put out of action in a duel with Quebec's cannon. Worst of all, the enlistment of Arnold's New Englanders would expire at the end of the year.

Montgomery had to attack.

On the night of December 30, under cover of a howling snowstorm, two sections of Americans moved against the city's Lower Town. Arnold, at the head of his 600 men, struck from the north. Montgomery, with 300, attacked from the south. And because General Carleton had foreseen that his enemy would strike at the Lower Town, where Quebec's defenses were weakest, both forces were blocked by British barricades.

In the north, Arnold was struck down with a bullet in his leg. Daniel Morgan took command, trying to rally his men to force the barricade. But Carleton sent a force of

200 men out another gate to cut off Morgan's rear. Struck by cannon shot and ball fired from behind them, the Americans began to surrender. Daniel Morgan fought on, roaring like a bull, until, forced back against a wall, he was finally compelled to surrender his sword to a priest. The northern strike had been routed.

To the south, Montgomery's smaller army had been fragmented by the storm and the city streets. Only about 90 were still with the American general when they came to the barricade. At once, his soldiers began sawing at the logs. Montgomery and Aaron Burr and other officers tore at the half-sawed logs with their hands. They got through. But then they came to a blockhouse. It held four little 3-pound cannon. The guns spoke. Richard Montgomery fell dying. Most of his officers were killed. Only Burr and a few others got away.

Montgomery's effort had failed. Yet Benedict Arnold did not allow the shattered little army to fall apart. Taking command of the 600 survivors, he returned to the Plains of Abraham, where he planted more guns and began a blockade of Quebec.

In the meantime, he called upon Congress for help. The defeat and death of Montgomery, however, had dismayed that body. It sent Arnold only 180 men, while dispatching a diplomatic commission to Quebec. Its members were Benjamin Franklin and Samuel Chase, two Protestants, and the Roman Catholic cousins, Charles Carroll of Carrollton and Father John Carroll. They tried to persuade the French-Canadians to join the patriot cause. But they failed, whereupon Congress changed its tactics back to force. Thousands of soldiers and a succession of generals were sent north, until, by the spring of 1776, there were as many as 8,000 patriots under General John Sullivan in Canada. If only half that number had marched north the previous summer, Canada would have certainly fallen to the patriots.

But too many had come too late. Sir Guy Carleton had wisely remained inside Quebec, allowing winter to work its worst on the Americans, hoping for a relieving fleet to come to his rescue in the spring. It did. In May the topsails of a British fleet carrying General John Burgoyne and a formidable army of British regulars and Hessian mercenaries could be seen on the St. Lawrence.

Canada had been saved for Britain, and the forces of the Revolution which had moved so gloriously north were to retreat in defeat to the south—where they remained for the rest of the war.

9

The Flag Flies at Moultrie

Probably the chief reason for the fatal slowness with which the American expeditions moved against Canada was that in the summer and fall of 1775 sentiment for reconciliation with Great Britain was still strong in the colonies.

Even such delegates to Congress as John Adams and Thomas Jefferson were hopeful of an end to the mutual slaughter of British subjects, and they were among those who approved the famous Olive Branch Petition which Congress sent to King George III. In this respectfully worded document, dated July 8, 1775, the delegates asked the king to find some means of effecting "a happy and permanent reconciliation."

His Majesty, however, refused to receive the petition. Speaking for the crown, Lord Suffolk told the American emissaries, "The King and his Cabinet are determined to listen to nothing from the illegal congress, to treat with the colonies only one by one, and in no event to recognize them in any form of association." The king himself made it plainer that August, when he proclaimed the colonies to be in a state of rebellion and called upon all his subjects to help "bring the traitors to justice." The following October, in his speech opening Parliament, he declared his intention "to bring a speedy end to these disorders."

When the king's words were reported back to America, they put an end to talk of reconciliation in Congress. They also angered many British leaders who favored some sort of compromise with the colonies. Almost at once a storm of opposition arose. Nevertheless, by a vote of more than two to one, Parliament approved the king's call for all-out war against the Americans. Mercenary troops were to be hired in Germany and sent to reinforce the British army in Boston.

That army, meanwhile, had been suffering grievously. Smallpox had broken out, and food was short. There were numerous desertions. General Sir William Howe, who had replaced Gage as the commander of British forces in the colonies, could count upon no more than 5,000 effective soldiers to defend the city.

George Washington, who was aware of this, yearned to attack his enemy. Twice, on September 11 and October 18, he proposed an assault. Each time, however, the council of war consisting of all his generals warned him against making the attempt.

This was because Washington was also having difficulties with his army. As fast as he recruited new soldiers, it seemed, expiring enlistments opened new gaps in his ranks. On December 1, insisting that their enlistments expired then, and not a month later, the Connecticut troops left camp. Enraged, Washington denounced the "dirty, mercenary spirit" of men upon whom he had depended and who had now "basely deserted the Cause of their Country." In January, he wrote: "The same desire of retiring into a chimney-corner seized the troops of New Hampshire, Rhode Island and Massachusetts as had worked upon those of Connecticut."

Much as Washington might complain, the truth was that these men *had* enlisted for only eight months and that they could not leave their farms and trades untended lest their families starve. Washington and most of his officers, wealthy men for the most part, were called upon to make no such sacrifices. In accordance with the customs of the times, these men believed that they had done their part—that they had completed the "campaign" they had " 'listed" for—and now it was up to someone else to step forward.

Fortunately, the resourceful Washington was always able to find "someone else." By January 16, with nearly 9,000 men fit for duty and another 1,500 ready to join, he felt strong enough to make his third proposal for an attack on Boston. Once again, the council of war opposed him. His generals agreed with Artemas Ward's suggestion that it would be safer for Washington to occupy Dorchester Heights. Moreover, Colonel Henry

Knox was expected to arrive almost any day with the artillery from Fort Ticonderoga. These invaluable cannon could be emplaced on the heights to command Boston. On January 24, Knox did bring the guns into Cambridge. There were sixty cannon in this "noble train of artillery," from 24-pound* cannon to little cohorns, or mortars, and Knox had brought them southeast to Boston by a heroic feat of transportation. By barge, sled, and sledge they had come, traversing the waterways of New York and the steep New England hills in the dead of a harsh American winter. When the barges sank, the guns were dredged up; when the sleds broke through the ice, they were fished up once more; and when oxen died in the traces or men broke their bones manhandling the cannon up and down snow-covered slopes, replacements were found to take their place.

The arrival of the artillery elated Washington and electrified the Continental Army. Sensing that the boredom of the siege was about to end, already incensed by news of the burning of Falmouth by the British and the destruction of Norfolk by Lord Dunmore, as well as inflamed by the ringing words of Tom Paine's *Common Sense*, Washington's soldiers set eagerly to work building the materials for fortification. They made wooden frames called chandeliers in which fascines—huge bundles of sticks bound together—could be placed and covered with earth. They also fashioned gabions—that is,

---

* In those days, cannon were rated by the weight of the ball they fired. Thus, a 24-pounder was not an artillery piece weighing only 24 pounds, but one weighing many tons firing a 24-pound ball.

wicker cylinders which could be filled with earth or sand. All these objects were to be emplaced upon the twin hills constituting Dorchester Heights.

On the night of March 2, 1776, the Americans began bombarding Boston. The cannonade was continued the following night, and in the darkness of March 4 it increased in fury. The British fired counterbattery, unaware that the American bombardment was only a distraction intended to conceal the true objective.

This was the heights, where a covering force of about 800 men had taken up positions. Behind them came a working party of some 1,200 men with more than 350 carts loaded with their gabions, chandeliers, and fascines. They also carried great bundles of hay weighing up to 800 pounds. These were dropped off the carts to form a screen, behind which the carts drove back and forth, unloading the fortification materials and bringing out the artillery. Meanwhile, an apple orchard was cut down and the trees used to form an abatis—that is, the tree trunks pointed inward toward the fort and the sharpened boughs pointing outward. Before daylight, Dorchester Heights had been occupied and fortified, and when the British awoke in Boston across the harbor, they found the American guns aimed down their throats. One astounded British officer wrote that the positions were made by "the Genii belonging to Aladdin's Wonder Lamp." General Howe, equally astounded, informed his superiors that they "must have been the employment of at least twelve thousand men."

Whatever their origin, they compelled Howe to call a

council of war, at which it was decided to evacuate Boston. On March 17, the last of perhaps 170 ships carrying Howe's soldiers and about 1,000 Tories sailed out of Boston Harbor, bound for Nantasket Harbor and thence to Halifax. Faint on the winds that blew them out to sea came the lamentations and angry rebukes of the Tories left behind. For them there was to be no mercy, and they knew it. In civil war—and the American Revolution was actually a civil war within the British Empire—no one hates as bitterly as brothers. Even the British whom the patriots had just driven from Boston were not despised as much as the loyalists. Thus, when the patriots triumphantly entered that city—then both the center and the symbol of the Revolution—it signaled the beginning of a long dark night for the Tories of America.

At the outbreak of the Revolution, perhaps as much as one-third of the people in America were Tories, or loyalists. Many of them were from the upper classes: doctors, merchants, lawyers, clergymen, landowners, or government officials. This is not to suggest, however, that the Revolution was a conflict between the rich loyalists and the poor rebels; between "haves" and "have-nots." Among the patriots there were also many people from the lower and middle classes.

Even democrats were drawn to the loyalist cause, especially the fiercely independent men of the western sections of the Southern states. These frontiersmen regarded the planters and merchants of the seaboard— leaders of the Revolution in the South such as George

Washington and Thomas Jefferson—as their oppressors. They resented the taxes imposed upon them without their consent and complained of the injustice of the courts. To them, the tyrant was not Britain but the Southern aristocrat.

Nevertheless, it seems safe to say that except for the South, the Revolution received more opposition than support from the gentry. The center of this opposition was in the Middle states: New York, New Jersey, Pennsylvania, Maryland, and Delaware. Considerably more than half of the "first people" in this area were Tories. They commanded a clear majority, and they were overcome only because they were inept and leaderless and up against a vigorous and organized minority.

Along with this Tory third of the population ranged against the patriots was another group—perhaps itself as large as a third—which remained aloof from the conflict. Many of these people were trimmers—that is, fence-sitters —who waited to see which way the war was going before they made their jump. To them, self-survival was the only objective. Their own personal well-being was more important than such ideals as liberty or justice. Thus, with the British they would pass as loyalist, and with the patriots they all were good rebels. They could toast George Washington or King George with equal ardor. In effect, they provided themselves with two sets of flags, waving one or the other depending on how the winds of military fortune were blowing.

Among the neutrals there were also those who opposed the war on the grounds of religious pacifism—that

111

is, a belief that the use of armed force is immoral. In the main, these neutrals were Quakers. Usually prosperous farmers and merchants, they were by nature conservative and inclined to favor the British cause.

In 1776 the Quakers voted to remain neutral, a position which angered the patriots. "In politics," John Adams growled, "the Middle Way is none at all." Although some Quakers did join the rebellion—notably General Greene and General Thomas Mifflin of Pennsylvania—the overwhelming bulk remained aloof. For this, they were hated as much as the loyalists. Moreover, they were suspected of being British spies and guides. Washington swore that he would hang any Quaker he found snooping about his camps, and so, much as they might protest their neutrality, they were actually regarded as Tories in disguise. As one patriot described a former friend of his: "A rigid old Quaker and of course a Damn'd Tory."

Yet, probably because of their claims to religious immunity, the Quakers escaped the general wrath which befell the Tories—actual or suspected—after the British were driven from Boston. From Maine to South Carolina, they were hunted down and routed out—lashed through the streets, tarred and feathered, pelted with rotten eggs, forced to go down on their knees to damn the king and bless the Revolution. Hatred of the Tories was without restraint. "A Tory is an incorrigible animal," wrote Governor Livingston of New Jersey, "and nothing but the extinction of life will extinguish his malevolence against liberty." Once again, Washington was for hanging the more notorious loyalists.

Unfortunately, as so often happens in the hysteria of the witch-hunt, many Tories more imagined than real were denounced to the authorities. Frequently, a man with a grudge or in debt would charge his innocent enemy or creditor with being a loyalist. In addition, informers were well rewarded. Unscrupulous men would not hesitate to make money by hailing an innocent man before a patriot committee. So general was the fear of these committees that one Tory complained: "I have had the misfortune to affront one of the Committee men, by not giving his Daughter a kiss. . . . This has offended the old man so much, that . . . he has several spyes to watch my actions. Sorry I did not give the ugly Jade a kiss."

Although the persecution of the Tories did not end in the bloodbaths typical of the French Revolution, it did include fines, imprisonment, exile, and, finally, confiscation of property. To Tom Paine, it was fitting that the land of the opposers of the Revolution should be distributed among needy patriots. The enemies of freedom would provide the economic basis for democracy.

Thus the witch-hunt continued, and yet, unpleasant as it may sound, the patriots actually had little choice. The Tories were their enemies, or at least the friends of their enemies. As civilians they were a dangerous fifth column operating in the rebel midst. At any time, they could change their civilian clothes for a British uniform, and the fact is that at one time there were nearly as many Tories serving General Howe as there were patriots in Washington's Continental Army. Finally, they were so successful in convincing Britain that the Revolution was the work of only a handful of malcontents that the minister who now directed the war from London actually believed that it would be won by Tory arms.

It was in November, 1775, that an exasperated King George placed Lord George Germain in charge of the war in North America. Although Germain was always answerable to Lord North and the cabinet, of which he was made a member, he was nevertheless given wide powers to conduct the American war.

Many Britons were astounded by the selection of George Germain. Here was a man who had been born with the proud name of Sackville, which he had changed in order to inherit a fortune. Here also was a former soldier who had been convicted of disobedience at the Battle of Minden and declared unfit to serve His Majesty in any military capacity whatever. And here he was, conducting the largest war so far in English history! To many historians, Lord George Germain was the worst high official to serve a British king. Others claim that this proud and lonely man was actually a dedicated and hardworking public servant who had been overwhelmed by an impossible task. However that may be, the fact is that Germain began his career by misjudging the strength of the Tories in America.

He believed that they controlled two-thirds of the people and were only waiting for the arrival of a British army strong enough to support them. As he said, he always strove "to engage the people of America in a cause which is equally their own and ours." Thus, British strategy—that is, the grand plan of conducting a war—was based on the belief that the Tories were waiting only for the signal to rise. That was why the first operation ordered by Germain was the expedition to Charleston.

Repeated messages from the fugitive governors of North Carolina, Virginia, and South Carolina "informed" his lordship of the presence of a huge number of loyalists in the South. With armed assistance, the governors said, the South could be reconquered for the king. Impressed, along with most of the cabinet, Germain collected about 2,500 troops and a large fleet. Sir Henry Clinton was to command the land force, and Sir Peter Parker was in charge at sea. The entire force was to sail on December 1, 1775. It would rendezvous some time in January, 1776, off Cape Fear, North Carolina. There the governor would provide a large force of loyalists, who would by then be in charge of the province.

Thus the plan, perfect on paper, until the seas and the storms began to shred it. On the Thames, high winds kept Sir Peter Parker's ships idle for four weeks. Then he sailed for Ireland to pick up most of the troops. There another five weeks elapsed before he was ready to sail again. Putting to sea on February 12, the fleet was scattered by a violent storm. The ships ran for the safety of the closest ports. Setting out again, they were once more sea-tossed and storm-blown, and it was not until the end of April—five months after the sailing date—that the British fleet at last made Cape Fear.

By then the loyalists of the interior had arisen—too soon. Without British arms to aid them, they were routed by the patriots at Moore's Creek Bridge. In the meantime, the delays that had thwarted the loyalist uprising gave the patriots enough time to fortify Charleston. Reinforcements from Virginia and North Carolina were rushed in. None other than General Charles Lee came down to take command. In all, Lee now had about 6,000 men to defend Charleston, when, on June 4, the sails of the British fleet rose above the horizon.

Most of this patriot force held down strong points and fortifications ringing the port city. But the key to Charleston was Sullivan's Island, to the north of the harbor. There Colonel William Moultrie had built a fort of palmetto logs. About 450 men, with thirty guns and not too much powder, guarded Fort Moultrie. Still, Colonel Moultrie was confident that the fort's palmetto logs, so far from splintering under British bombardment, would soak up cannonballs like a sponge.

Out on the water, Sir Henry Clinton thought he could take Fort Moultrie by land assault. Opposite the fort on Sullivan's Island was Long Island. It was separated from Sullivan's by a narrow strip of water called the Breach. Clinton thought his men could wade the Breach and storm Fort Moultrie. So he landed a force there in what was to be a probing operation—that is, to probe the American strength, feel it out, and, if it was found to be weak, to strike hard at the weak point.

On June 28, Clinton put 500 men ashore on Long Island. Redcoats ran to the Breach and jumped in. To their officers' horror, many of these heavily laden soldiers vanished in holes seven feet deep. When boats were put into the water, they ran aground in shallows. The Breach was not a ford, but an impassable moat—so the British decided to bombard Fort Moultrie into submission. The battle for Charleston became a fight between a fleet and a fort.

Nine warships sailed to battle stations. From the bomb ketch *Thunder* came the first shots. They fell short. Rather than work in closer and perhaps collide with other ships, *Thunder*'s skipper ordered the powder charges in his mortars doubled. They were—and the overcharges broke the mortar beds. *Thunder* was useless.

Now the Americans began firing back. Patriot gunners sighted in on Sir Peter Parker's flagship, *Bristol*. They shot away her cable, and as she drifted end on toward the fort, they raked her. Twice, *Bristol*'s quarterdeck was cleared of everyone but Parker. Then, to the admiral's deep embarrassment, the Americans shot off the seat of his trousers and singed his behind. Next, Colonel Moultrie's men put *Experiment* out of action.

Nevertheless, the British maintained their cannonade. Broadside after broadside shook the fort. Once three or perhaps even four broadsides struck it simultaneously,

117

shaking it so badly that Moultrie feared another such salvo might knock it down. Yet the palmetto logs held, actually soaking up so many balls that the sides of the fort looked like cobblestone streets.

Now the roaring of the artillery duel rose in crescendo. Inside the fort, the heat from the powder flashes and the hot sun overhead was almost unbearable. Ashore, soldiers and civilians alike gazed anxiously at the tiny square of logs. Suddenly they gasped. The flag had been shot away! Was the fort surrendering? From the British ships came a cheer. From the shore, a groan.

Within the fort, a sergeant named Jasper cried, "Colonel, don't let us fight without our flag!" Moultrie shrugged and answered, "What can you do? The staff is broke."

In reply, Sergeant Jasper dashed outside the fort, a sponge staff in his hand. While cannonballs shrieked and crashed around him, he seized the fallen flag, affixed it to the staff, and set it upright again. Now it was the Charleston shore that cheered to see the blue flag with its white crescent and the word "Liberty" whipping in the breeze again.

Dismayed, the British tried to move in closer. Three ships upped anchor to move around the western end of the island. There they could deliver a flanking fire—that is, from the side. But all three ships ran aground. Two of them worked free, but one, *Actaeon*, was caught. As night fell, the American gunners turned on *Actaeon* and set her afire.

Those were the last shots of the Battle of Charleston.

About an hour before midnight, the British fleet slipped its cables and set its sails for the open sea. Fort Moultrie had held, Charleston was saved—and it would be two years before the South would see the sails of a British fleet again.

10

Disaster at Brooklyn Heights

When General Gage wrote to London to inform his superiors of the difficulties of crushing the rebellion, he had specified that a force of at least 50,000 troops would be required. Naturally, Gage was aware that the entire British army numbered barely 50,000 men and that most of them were needed to garrison Britain's outposts around the world. So he had suggested that the crown hire mercenaries, recommending Russia as one possible source.

For a time, Britain was hopeful that Catherine the Great would supply 20,000 soldiers for the American war, but then, the czarina changed her mind. Desperate for manpower, King George turned to Germany, the birthplace of his grandfather and the land which gave Britain its ruling House of Hanover. There the king

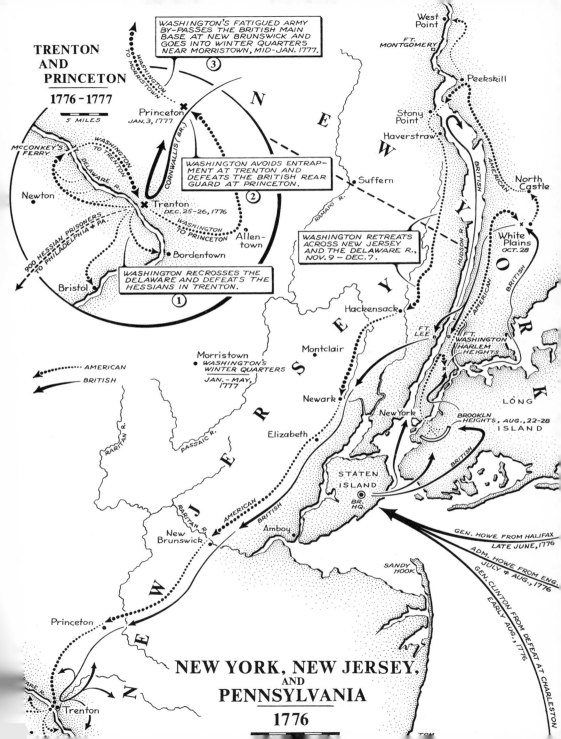

TRENTON AND PRINCETON

1776 – 1777

5 MILES

WASHINGTON'S FATIGUED ARMY BY-PASSES THE BRITISH MAIN BASE AT NEW BRUNSWICK AND GOES INTO WINTER QUARTERS NEAR MORRISTOWN, MID-JAN. 1777.
③

WASHINGTON AVOIDS ENTRAPMENT AT TRENTON AND DEFEATS THE BRITISH REAR GUARD AT PRINCETON.
②

WASHINGTON RECROSSES THE DELAWARE AND DEFEATS THE HESSIANS IN TRENTON.
①

WASHINGTON TO MORRISTOWN

Princeton
JAN. 3, 1777

McCONKEY'S FERRY

WASHINGTON TO TRENTON

DELAWARE R.

CORNWALLIS (BR.)

Newton

Trenton
DEC. 25-26, 1776

WASHINGTON TO PRINCETON

Allen-town

Bordentown

900 HESSIAN PRISONERS TO PHILADELPHIA * PA.

Bristol

WASHINGTON RETREATS ACROSS NEW JERSEY AND THE DELAWARE R., NOV. 9 – DEC. 7.

West Point

FT. MONTGOMERY

Peekskill

Stony Point

Haverstraw

North Castle

Suffern

RAMAPO R.

BRITISH

AMERICAN

HUDSON R.

White Plains
OCT. 28

BRITISH

Hackensack

FT. LEE

FT. WASHINGTON
HARLEM HEIGHTS

Morristown
WASHINGTON'S WINTER QUARTERS JAN. – MAY, 1777

Montclair

Newark

•••••••• AMERICAN

———— BRITISH

RARITAN R.

PASSAIC R.

Elizabeth

New York

BROOKLYN HEIGHTS, AUG., 22-28
ISLAND

LONG

RARITAN R.

AMERICAN

BRITISH

New Brunswick

Amboy

STATEN ISLAND

BR. HQ.

BRITISH

SANDY HOOK

GEN. HOWE FROM HALIFAX
LATE JUNE, 1776

ADM. HOWE FROM ENG.
JULY # AUG., 1776

GEN. CLINTON FROM
EARLY AUG., 1776

DEFEAT AT CHARLESTON

Princeton

Trenton

NEW YORK, NEW JERSEY,
AND
PENNSYLVANIA

1776

found all the hired soldiers he would need. They came from various principalities: Brunswick, Waldeck, Anhalt-Zerbst, Anspach-Beyreuth, Hesse-Hanau, Hesse-Cassel. Before the war was over, some 30,000 German mercenaries would have served the British crown, and because more than half of them were provided by the Landgrave of Hesse-Cassel, all came to be called Hessians.

Britain agreed to pay all the soldiers' expenses, in addition to $35 for each soldier killed or $12 for each wounded man. To the Landgrave of Hesse-Cassel alone, it contracted to pay more than $500,000 a year for the "rental" of his troops.

In those days, there was nothing unusual in such an arrangement. This was still the era of limited war fought by small professional armies at the command of kings. All of a king's subjects were not liable to military service. Ambitious noblemen or gentlemen were the officers, and the ranks were filled with men who sought the soldier's calling as an alternative to jail or starvation. Even though the patriots in Washington's army were, in effect, the first citizen-soldiers to appear since the days of the Roman Republic, the true democratic army had to await the coming of the French Revolution. In a democracy, everyone would be liable to service, and this would make possible the mass draft armies of the present. Thus, when King George hired mercenary troops, he was doing only what every other king would have done in his position.

The Americans, however, could not forgive him. To

hire foreigners to fight a foreign foe was one thing, but to hire them to fight Americans, in effect the blood brothers or cousins of the British, that was something else again—something despicable. Now the catalogue of King George's crimes was complete. The colonies wanted no part of him or Britain. Now, in that historic summer of 1776, they wanted freedom—independence pure and simple. And so, as Congress convened again, Thomas Jefferson approached John Adams with the suggestion that he write a declaration of American independence. Adams declined. Surprised, Jefferson asked, "What can be your reasons?"

"Reason first," Adams answered, "you are a Virginian, and a Virginian ought to appear at the head of this business. Reason second, I am obnoxious, suspected and unpopular. You are very much otherwise. Reason third, you can write ten times better than I can."

"Well," said Jefferson, "if you are decided, I will do as well as I can."

With that, the youthful red-haired delegate from Virginia set to work on his great battle cry of liberty. Much of what he wrote was deleted, of course, particularly his savage attack on King George. Jefferson, a rich slaveholder, also denounced the institution of slavery, but this was taken out as well. On July 4, 1776, the Declaration of Independence was adopted.

First to sign the document was John Hancock. Writing his name with a big, bold flourish, Hancock remarked, "There, I guess King George will be able to read that!"

123

After him came the others, fifty-six delegates, pledging to each other "our Lives, our Fortunes, and our sacred Honor." The Adamses of Massachusetts signed, beaming, delighted that "the river is passed, and the bridge cut away." So did the Lees of Virginia and Jefferson himself. Wealthy Charles Carroll of Carrollton, the only Catholic to sign the Declaration, affixed his name because "I had in view not only our independence of England, but the toleration of all sects professing the Christian religion." And of course, Benjamin Franklin was in line. "We must all hang together, or assuredly we shall all hang separately," he had quipped, thereby reminding all the delegates that if the Revolution failed, their heads would likely decorate the balcony of Independence Hall. And so, four days later, the Declaration of Independence was published in America.

Up and down the seaboard, news of the Declaration was greeted with ringing bells and bonfires. In Savannah, King George was burned in effigy. In New York his statue was pulled down, in Connecticut his leaden image was melted down for bullets, and in Boston a crowd tore the king's coat of arms from the statehouse and burned it. And so, with freedom declared by Congress, it was now up to the Continental Army to defend it.

British strategy for the campaign of 1776 had shifted from Boston to New York City. Possession of New York, it was believed by both Lord Germain and General Howe, was vital. The city sat midway among the colonies, and its capture would split the Americans in two.

Also, once Howe had taken New York, he could move up the broad Hudson to join another force moving south from Canada. When this happened, the British would have opened the back door to New England.

The Americans, meanwhile, were very much aware of where the blow would fall. Confident as ever, the British had boasted openly about their plans. Thus forewarned, the Americans had to face the critical decision of whether or not to attempt to defend New York. Situated as it was on an island, the city was highly vulnerable— and especially to sea power. A British fleet could easily sail up the Hudson and cut off the American rear. Yet to abandon the city would have disastrous effect upon patriot morale. Both Congress and General Washington were convinced of this, and so it was decided to hold New York.

Throughout the spring and summer of 1776, some 10,000 patriots worked on the city's fortifications. The emphasis was on big guns which would keep the British fleet at bay. Almost every island and hill, it seemed, blossomed with a redoubt or a barricaded cannon. As a result, Washington's command of about 19,000 men was unwisely dispersed over the area. Eventually, however, the American commander Washington brought a third of his force over to Long Island and placed them under General Nathanael Greene. At once, this energetic general began constructing works on Brooklyn Heights. Like Dorchester Heights below Boston, Brooklyn Heights commanded Manhattan Island. It would be impossible to take New York City, then, without first taking Long Island and evicting the Americans from Brooklyn Heights.

Of this, Sir William Howe was well aware when the fleet commanded by his brother, Admiral Lord Richard "Black Dick" Howe, brought his army into New York Harbor. Nevertheless, he did not immediately land on Long Island. Instead, to the patriots' astonishment, he put his men ashore on Staten Island across the Narrows. That was on July 2, and for almost two more months the British war chief sat idle on Staten Island. His inactivity baffled Washington. What were the British waiting for? The answer, of course, was that the wary, slow-moving Howe was waiting for camping equipment. With more than 30,000 men at his command, including Sir Henry Clinton's woebegone force up from Charleston, he would not move until he had the ovens, kettles, tentage, and other gear which were considered vital to the professional armies of the day. In the meantime, the delighted Washington took advantage of the delay to strengthen Brooklyn Heights.

Unfortunately, however, the Americans were still thinking in terms of Bunker Hill. They expected that the British would make another frontal assault, which they would once again deal a bloody repulse. Such thinking received further emphasis after General Greene became ill and General Putnam, one of the heroes of Bunker Hill, took command. Accordingly, no attempt was made to oppose the British when they began landing on Long Island. Instead, Putnam expected the enemy to march up the main road straight into his guns. There his right was held by about 1,700 men under General "Lord" Stirling* and his left by his main body under General Sullivan. To the rear, guarding Brooklyn, was his reserve.

Sir William Howe, however, had no intention of repeating Bunker Hill. He had learned of the existence of unguarded secondary roads in the American rear, and he intended to use them. He would turn the American left—that is, get behind Sullivan and into the enemy rear.

Howe's left was led by Major General James Grant, a Yankee hater who had once boasted he would make women of all American males. He was to attack Stirling and hold him in place—that is, keep him occupied. Howe's center was composed of Hessians under General Philip de Heister. They were to strike at Sullivan. In the meantime, Howe was to take his own main body wide around the American left. At dark on August 26, guided by Tories, Howe's troops moved out. They were making for the unguarded Jamaica Pass leading into the Jamaica Road and Sullivan's unsuspecting rear. At dawn of August 27, 1776, they reached it—firing two cannon as a signal that they had successfully turned the American left.

Also at dawn, General Grant's troops began attacking Stirling. The Americans fought back stubbornly. Stirling had told them what Grant thought of American

---

* William Alexander, "Lord Stirling," is probably the only nobleman in American history, although his claim to the earldom of Stirling was rejected by the House of Lords.

men, and they struck at his troops savagely. Stirling, of course, was not aware that Grant only wanted to keep him engaged.

Now General de Heister heard Howe's two cannon shots. At once he ordered his Hessians forward. Bands playing, some of the soldiers singing hymns, the Hessians moved toward Sullivan's men. Their long, slender bayonets were outthrust before them. Striding confidently, their tall brass miters rising two feet above their heads, they were an awesome sight. Still, the Americans resisted them stubbornly—until word was received that the British were in their rear. With this, Sullivan's men panicked. They turned to run, and the Hessians drove their bayonets into their backs. Told that Americans gave no quarter, the Hessians made a merciless havoc, sometimes spitting the rebels on trees or slaughtering entire groups of men who had thrown down their arms. Of course, some Americans had feigned surrender, waiting until the Hessians came up to them before opening fire, and because of this trick, the Hessians—and the English, too—killed every rebel in sight, even when the Americans begged for mercy.

On the American right, Stirling's men fought on—until young Lord Cornwallis led a British detachment into their own rear. Struck from behind, by Grant to their right, and by the Hessians on their left, the Americans broke. Many of them drowned attempting to escape through the Gowanus marshes. Others scattered into the woods. Stirling himself surrendered to the Hessians rather than submit to the odious Grant.

All that remained now for a decisive British victory, perhaps even the destruction of Washington's army and the end of the war, was to storm the main redoubt on Brooklyn Heights. Only a frightened reserve stood in Howe's way. Yet he hesitated. His path to glory was barred only by a ditch one mile long and three or four feet deep, an obstacle which the scornful General James Robertson snorted would not have stopped a fox hunter —and he did not advance. His officers were pleading for the order to attack, and the blood of his men was up— they wanted to massacre "Mr. Washington and his dirty pack of New England long-faces"—and Howe halted them. Why he did will never be known. Perhaps he could not forget Bunker Hill. Much later, appearing before Parliament, he testified that he had not been able to scout the American position thoroughly. He feared that there might be more enemy works behind the ones he faced. Whatever the reason, General Howe halted his victorious army and began to dig approaches toward Brooklyn Heights.

The next morning the heartsore General George Washington looked out toward the enemy—and his heart leaped. The British were digging trenches! They would not storm the heights which he had come over to Brooklyn to command! Here was a wonderful chance to save his army, and the next day he called a council of war at which it was decided to evacuate Long Island.

It was a desperate gamble. To Washington's front, a British army was steadily drawing closer. To his rear, a British fleet rode at anchor only a few miles away. All

129

depended on the weather and the skill of John Glover's regiment from Marblehead.

Although these soldiers were on the rolls as infantry, they were actually men of the sea. They walked with a sailor's rolling gait, and their blue pea jackets and loose white jackets belied the soldier's cocked hat on their heads. On the night of August 29, together with similar sea soldiers from the Salem regiment, they manned the fleet of small boats which Washington had wisely collected in advance. Bringing them up to the Brooklyn ferry landing on the East River, they quietly took aboard the army that had deliberately left its campfires burning to deceive the British. Now they would have to run the gauntlet of the British fleet. But no—a strong wind had sprung up to keep the enemy ships out of the river. Then, providentially, a heavy fog settled on the water, concealing the passage of the American army from the eyes of the British lookouts.

By dawn the American rear guard had taken ship and was embarked for New York, and it was only then that Sir William Howe discovered that Washington had escaped.

11

The Long Retreat

One explanation of Sir William Howe's failure to crush the Americans at Brooklyn Heights is his supposed sympathy for the patriots and his reluctance to shed the blood of his American brothers.

This claim has not, of course, been proved. Yet the fact remains that both Sir William and his lordly brother had come to America as the king's peace commissioners. Both the Howes, being Whigs, had opposed King George's war policy. The only reason they had been chosen to command on both land and sea in America was that they were the ranking officers in their respective services. Sir William, needing money, had been less reluctant than his brother to accept the charge. Even so, he still seems to have thought it necessary to apologize in Parliament to his Whig colleagues.

Lord Richard Howe had flatly refused to command the British fleet unless he was given the power to make peace with the colonies. As a result, both he and his brother had been made peace commissioners. Actually, their powers were limited. They could only promise pardons. They could not treat with Congress, because the king recognized no such body. They could not even look upon Washington as a general. Thus, Lord Howe wrote to the American commander as "Mr." Washington. Told that no such person lived in the American camp, he next addressed a letter to "George Washington, Esquire," and this was coldly refused.

After the Battle of Long Island, however, with adverse tides making a waterborne invasion of New York City temporarily impossible, the Howes tried another tack. The captured General Sullivan was released on parole to go to Philadelphia to inform Congress that Lord Howe would be delighted to receive a delegation to talk of peace. However, he specified that the Congressmen could only be received as private citizens. The Howes could not recognize Congress.

To the dismay of radicals such as the Adamses, there were many Congressmen who favored accepting Lord Howe's proposal. They argued that if Congress flatly turned down any such overtures, it might be branded as a warmongering body. Better to demonstrate once and for all that there was really no hope of peace with Britain, they said, and so Congress named Benjamin Franklin, John Adams, and Edward Rutledge as a committee of three to confer with Lord Howe.

Once aboard the admiral's flagship in New York Harbor, they were treated to a meal of "good claret, good bread, cold ham, tongue, and mutton," after which they were ushered into his lordship's presence. Courteous and friendly, Admiral Lord Howe nevertheless made it clear that he could promise nothing but the hope of pardons. Although he gave his own assurances that all would go well with the colonies, he admitted that he could not even pledge that Parliament would not try to tax them again. In other words, the colonies would just have to trust in the goodwill of Britain. Thus, Lord Howe was not offering peace but only asking for unconditional surrender. He could not, he told his three visitors, even receive them as members of Congress, because his sovereign recognized no such body. To this, John Adams replied that he and his colleagues were perfectly willing to be received "in any Capacity his Lordship pleased, except *in that of British subjects.*" His patience strained, the admiral observed that he felt for America as a brother, and, if America should fall, he should lament it "like the loss of a brother." To this Benjamin Franklin dryly retorted, "My Lord, we will do our utmost endeavors to save your lordship that mortification." Upon that thrust, the meeting broke up.

Peace talk had been put aside, and now, reaching for the sword once more, the Howe brothers resolved to attack New York.

Although Washington's evacuation of Long Island was one of the most brilliant feats in his military career, his reputation would seldom sink lower. "Would to heaven General Lee were here is the language of officers and men," wrote John Haslet, the colonel commanding the Delaware regiment. Moreover, the troops had lost faith not only in their commander in chief but themselves as well. Bunker Hill was forgotten, and the prowess of the riflemen was made into a mockery. Because the rifle was slow in firing and could not hold a bayonet, it had been useless at Brooklyn Heights. Disillusioned with the riflemen, who would eventually be disbanded as a corps, American officers now urged Congress to provide a musket two inches longer than the British Brown Bess. This would give the patriots an advantage in bayonet fighting, now dolefully recognized as the true arbiter of battle.

Such were the lessons learned in the Battle of Long Island. And yet the most important one, the folly of trying to hold an island in the face of British sea power, seemed to be lost on General Washington. Hardly had his men gained the safety of Manhattan Island before he began preparations to defend the city. Half his top commanders—notably General Greene—warned him against holding New York. Greene argued that the city was two-thirds Tory as it was, so why not burn it and withdraw to a more defensible position? Washington, however, decided to carry out Congress' instructions not to destroy New York.

Thus, he had a force in readiness at Kip's Bay (present-day East Thirty-fourth Street) when the British began landing there on September 15. To his intense dismay, however, the Americans fled the moment the British warships in the East River began to bombard them. Infuriated, Washington rode to the battlefront.

"Take the walls!" he roared at his fleeing soldiers. "Take the cornfield!"

A few sheepish men obeyed, but the rest flowed around their tall commander in chief in a frightened flood. Fear of the dreadful British bayonets was too powerful, and no matter how often Washington aimed his pistol at them or flailed with his cane or sword, they kept on running. Dashing his hat on the ground, Washington bellowed, "Are these the men with whom I am to defend America?" So great was his anger that he paid no heed to the approach of a party of Hessians and might have fallen captive—had not an aide seized his bridle and led him away.

Once again, Sir William Howe had a golden chance. If he struck straight across the island, he would cut off 4,000 rebel soldiers under Israel Putnam in Lower Manhattan. Instead, careful as ever, chary of British lives, satisfied with obtaining his first day's objective, he halted for the night. In the meantime, Putnam's force rejoined the American main body in Harlem. The next day Howe swung to his right, or north, to attack Washington again. A short but hot two-hour battle ensued, with the Americans showing a surprising change of heart and actually sallying out of their entrenchments to attack the British and drive them back.

Nevertheless, the southern end of Manhattan Island, what was then considered New York City, was firmly in

British hands. And the Tories who had remained behind gave them a warm welcome. When the redcoats marched down Broadway, swarms of loyalists—women included —hoisted British officers on their shoulders and paraded them around in triumph. Two women pulled down the American flag from the fort and hoisted the Union Jack in its place. New York, it seemed, was going to provide the British army with the sort of pleasant headquarters which they had missed in Boston. But then a group of patriots, who had hidden themselves when the British arrived, set fire to the city.

Breaking out in three different places, the fire raged out of control. Because the fire company had been disbanded, there was no organization to fight it, and with the fire engines out of order, even makeshift firemen could do no good. Moreover, Washington had removed all the church bells and melted them down for cannon, so no alarms were rung. Nevertheless, British soldiers and seamen fell frantically to work pulling down houses in the path of the roaring blaze. Fortunately for them, the wind changed as the devouring flames reached Broadway, and only one-third of the city was destroyed.

That was enough, however, to make life uncomfortable for the conquerors. One officer complained of being cramped "like herrings in a barrel," and Sir William Howe was still infuriated at the "Yankee plot," when, the day after the fire, a captive patriot spy was brought into his presence.

Nathan Hale had been captured on Long Island, where he had been observing enemy troop movements for General Washington. Questioned by Howe, he freely admitted this activity. Without even the formality of a drumhead court, Howe curtly ordered Nathan Hale to be hanged. When the prisoner requested the consolation of a Bible and a clergyman in his few remaining hours, he was refused. A gallows was speedily erected at what is now Fifty-second Street just east of First Avenue. Without a trace of fear, Hale mounted the scaffold, standing calm and composed while the noose was curled around his neck. His last words were "I only regret that I have but one life to lose for my country." Then the hangman tightened the noose.

Now that Howe held New York City it was imperative that Sir Guy Carleton move south from Canada into New York State. When this happened, and Howe drove north to meet him, a line of steel would have been drawn between New England and the rest of the colonies. This, of course, was at the heart of British strategy for the reconquest of the colonies, and this was why Carleton rather than Howe had received the bulk of reinforcements in the spring of 1776.

Yet this normally decisive and bold commander did not move rapidly. First, with 13,000 men at his command, he failed to trap the demoralized patriot army that retreated from Quebec. Next, he allowed most of the summer to pass waiting to be supplied with a lakes fleet that never came. British shipyards, already overworked providing landing equipment for General Howe, were unable to supply Carleton.

Thus, it was not until the end of August that Carleton was able to assemble a fleet of nearly 700 flat-bottomed boats to transport his infantry, plus a battle fleet of three schooners, a floating battery, a gondola, and a dozen gunboats. All told, Carleton's gunfire ships mounted ninety guns. Putting out on Lake Champlain in early October, Carleton made for Fort Ticonderoga at the southern end.

Opposing him was a makeshift fleet commanded by Benedict Arnold. At first, the Americans had been ready to abandon Ticonderoga, but the audacious Arnold had changed their minds. At a conference held in July, Arnold had convinced General Horatio Gates that the vital fort could be held. On Gates' orders, he began building a fleet of galleys and gundalows manned by soldiers drawn from Gates' regiments. In all, Arnold's force of about a dozen vessels could discharge only about half the weight of metal in Carleton's fleet. Nevertheless, Arnold also put out on the lake in early October, taking up station off Valcour Island about fifty miles north of Ticonderoga.

There, on October 11, Carleton's superior force discovered him—and gave battle. Although outnumbered and outgunned, the Americans fought stubbornly. Arnold himself aimed the guns of his flagship, *Congress*, until that unstable craft became riddled and afire and had to be abandoned. Still, the Americans fought on— exchanging shot and ball at musket range, raked by Carleton's Indians firing from the shore. But they were routed. One by one Arnold's ships were sunk, and the six which escaped back to Crown Point finally had to be burned.

Crown Point also was abandoned, as Arnold led his survivors back to Ticonderoga. Now, it seemed, a lightning stroke by Carleton would recapture the fort and reopen the gateway to the Hudson. He would have had little opposition. The Americans holding it were so demoralized that they allowed British foraging parties to drive off 150 head of cattle without lifting a finger to stop them. Carleton dawdled, however. Then the weather broke. Rather than risk a campaign in the cruel northern winter, the British chief withdrew from Lake Champlain, even abandoning Crown Point.

Thus, Arnold's desperate stand at Valcour Island had wrecked British plans for a junction on the Hudson in 1776.

George Washington still seemed to favor Bunker Hill tactics. After the defeat at Kip's Bay, he had occupied Harlem Heights, where Howe had been unable to dislodge him. Then, gaining respect for enemy sea power, he had moved to the mainland and built another formidable position at Kingsbridge. When the slow-moving Howe at last marched out of New York to get around him, Washington retreated again—this time to an even stronger position in White Plains. Once again, the "Old Fox," as some of the younger British officers were beginning to call Washington, was sitting on a hilltop waiting for the British to charge into his guns.

His reasons were twofold. First, he was outnumbered,

139

25,000 to 14,000; second, he still could not trust his troops to confront the British in open battle. He knew that the Americans fought best from behind entrenchments. Many of his troops were militia, who, in his words, "were continually coming and going without rendering the least Earthly Service." Worse than the rank and file, however, were his junior officers. Most of these—the bitter, outspoken Washington complained— were "a parcel of ignorant, stupid men, who might make tolerable soldiers but who are bad officers." Because of these shortcomings in the number and quality of his troops, Washington refused to give battle on any terms but his own. " 'Tis our business to study to avoid any considerable misfortune," said General Greene, "and to take post where the enemy will be obliged to fight us, and not we them."

General Howe was aware of this. Yet it goaded him to find that he, one of Europe's most respected professionals, was repeatedly being outmaneuvered by this amateur.

Thus, finding himself at White Plains once again looking up at Washington on a hill, Sir William Howe decided to attack. A force of British and Hessians moved against the hill frontally in a feint, while Hessians under Colonel Johann Rall struck at the American right. Rall, however, did not get into position in time, and the Americans were able to roll back the frontal thrust. Reforming, Howe ordered the same assault forward, and this time Rall successfully put himself on the American right flank. Rather than let him move into his rear, Washington abandoned his position on Chatterton's Hill and moved to another height of land.

Here, once again, Howe dawdled. He might have moved quickly before the Americans could entrench themselves in their new position. But he did not. During the delay heavy rains made a renewed assault impossible, and Washington again took advantage of the respite to withdraw to a new and stronger position at North Castle behind the Croton River.

At this point Washington unwisely divided his forces. He left his main body of 7,000 men under General Lee at North Castle, sent 5,000 under General Greene into New Jersey to guard against a thrust at Philadelphia, and took 4,000 up the Hudson to Peekskill to protect the Highlands. Meanwhile, another 3,000 men were in Fort Washington at the north end of Manhattan Island. For a time Washington thought of abandoning this post. But the advice of Greene, plus the instructions of Congress, changed his mind. And in this, he gave his frustrated opponent the opportunity that he sought so eagerly.

Informed by a deserter of the plans of Fort Washington, Howe moved to take the fortress the patriots thought was impregnable. On November 13 he appeared outside its walls and summoned it to surrender. If it did not capitulate, he warned, he would slaughter the entire garrison. Colonel Robert Magaw, commanding Fort Washington, confident of its strength, scornfully refused. On November 14, Howe began bombarding the fort from floating batteries in the Harlem River and a warship in the Hudson. Then he ordered about 13,000 men to attack it in four columns.

For a while the Americans fought bravely. Their outposts took a heavy toll among the Hessians advancing with drums beating and oboes wailing. Nevertheless, the weight of British arms drove them back inside the fort. To his horror, Colonel Magaw realized that his overcrowded position might soon be turned into a slaughter pen. Enemy artillery could make a bloodbath of Fort Washington. So Magaw surrendered. To the intense anger of the Hessians—and many British officers—Howe accepted the American surrender. By the rules of war then accepted, he could have put the entire garrison to the sword, as he had threatened to do. No one would have held him accountable. As one indignant British officer said, he would then "have struck such a panic as would have prevented the Congress from ever being able to raise another Army."

Nevertheless, the loss of nearly 3,000 men as prisoners was shock enough for both Congress and General Washington. So was the loss of scores of cannon and thousands of shot, shell, and muskets. Even without the slaughter of the garrison, the capitulation of Fort Washington dealt the patriot cause a severe setback which was at once moral and material.

As though energized by his victory, Howe moved swiftly, sending Lord Cornwallis across the Hudson to trap Greene at Fort Lee. Greene got away, but he had to leave his guns behind—and now the British bag rose to 146 cannon, 12,000 shot and shell, 2,800 muskets, 400,-000 rounds of ball—and an abundance of camping equipment. Scenting another victory, Cornwallis pursued Greene to Hackensack, where he had joined Washington. Together, the Americans began their miserable flight across New Jersey to the Delaware River.

It was now late November, and the fall rains had turned the roads into a mire. Through the cold slop of mud and the chill November downpour slogged the retreating Americans. At every stop, Washington fired off letters to General Lee imploring him to join him with the main body. Lee, however, did not budge from North Castle.

Onward across New Jersey—soaked, starved, stumbling—Washington's men retreated. "No lads ever shewed greater activity in retreating than we," one of the soldiers wrote sardonically. ". . . Our Soldiers are the best fellows in the World at this business." As they fell back toward the Delaware, their numbers rapidly decreased. Another soldier wrote: "About 2,000 of us have been obliged to run damn'd hard before abt. 10,000 of the Enemy."

Even in retreat, however, the patriots showed their ingenuity. As they fell back, they destroyed the bridges they had crossed. Wherever he could, Washington pretended to be preparing to make a stand, thus compelling Lord Cornwallis to exercise caution. Fearful of ambush, at which the Indian-fighting patriots were adept, the

British scoured the woods or brought up artillery at the slightest sign of rebel opposition. Thus, it took them nineteen days to cover seventy-four miles.

Meanwhile, Sir William Howe, who had been romantically admiring the scenery in and around New York City, which he believed superior to anything he had seen in Italy, suddenly remembered that his plans also called for the capture of Newport, Rhode Island. Withdrawing some of the troops under Cornwallis, he gave them to Sir Henry Clinton, who took Newport without a fight on December 8.

Now the sluggish British commander in chief decided to join Cornwallis, whose advance units had reached the Delaware River just as the last of the patriot rear guards crossed the river. To the chagrin of both generals, Washington had wisely collected or burned all the boats along seventy-five miles of the river. The British could not cross, at least not immediately.

Worse, the patriots had also concentrated artillery on the opposite bank. When Sir William Howe appeared on the Jersey side in person, he was received by the combined firepower of nearly forty cannon. Without boats, confronted by artillery, and anxious anyway to be back in comfortable quarters in New York, Sir William Howe decided it was too late to invade Philadelphia.

Instead, he would winter in New York and deliver the knockout blow next spring.

12

The Revolution Rallies

The month of December, 1776, was the month of crisis for the patriots.

Following the loss of Fort Washington and the flight of General Washington's army across New Jersey, the Middle states of New York, Pennsylvania, and New Jersey all but defected from the rebel cause.

In New Jersey, the vital land link between New York City and the patriot capital in Philadelphia, swarms of so-called rebels renounced the patriot cause. They accepted Howe's offer of pardon and took loyalty oaths to King George. Many of them enrolled in Tory units to fight their former comrades. Meanwhile, the farmers of New Jersey, whom Washington had asked to scorch the earth in front of the British, instead gave the enemy a gay greeting and gladly sold them meat and produce.

In New York City, jubilant loyalists tried to outdo one another in making the British army welcome. Their guests, meanwhile, were so confident of victory that officers in the British mess were openly predicting that the rebellion would be crushed by Christmas. "This business is pretty near over," wrote Lord Percy. Lord Cornwallis, meanwhile, prepared to return to England. It seemed to him that all the fighting in America was over and that an ambitious young nobleman such as himself should hurry home to seek an assignment to other fields of glory and promotion.

Sir William Howe thought so little of rebel strength that he was content to hold New Jersey with a chain of posts. As few as 3,000 Hessians under Colonel Carl von Donop faced Washington's army across the Delaware. They held a six-mile line from Bordentown up to Trenton and Howe thought they were strong enough to keep the Americans in check throughout the winter.

The presence of the Hessians across the river seemed to magnify the hysteria that gripped Pennsylvania. Most of that state appeared ready to go over to the enemy. Only a handful of merchants and farmers would accept Continental currency because they feared that the British would declare it worthless. In Philadelphia, as the population dwindled, the mayor cordially invited the British to dine with him. Threatened by angry patriots, the mayor hastily left town—but then, so did most of the patriots. Shops were closed, and only people with gloomy faces walked the streets. Although some brave souls plannned a house-to-house defense of the city, this plan was abandoned after Congress also fled the capital. On December 10, Congress had boldly proclaimed its unshakable belief in the American people, calling upon all patriots to stand firm. Two days later its members meekly departed for Baltimore.

Even the military were despondent, and many officers were inclined to blame General Washington for their predicament. History has shown, of course, that Washington's series of defeats and retreats from Long Island to Pennsylvania were actually a series of masterful "delaying actions." Washington had traded blood and ground for time—and time was the most valuable. Time would give him another day on which to fight, and it was for this that he had saved his army. So long as his army remained in being, the Revolution was alive. Some —perhaps many—of his compatriots did not see it this way, however. They could not forget that single hour of glory at Bunker Hill—in which Washington had had no part—and everything else by comparison seemed disgraceful. Thus, even some of the Continental Army's ranking officers were critical of Washington.

Chief among them was General Charles Lee, who had finally begun leading Washington's main body—now down to 2,700 men—south from North Castle. In New Jersey, two days' march from Pennsylvania, he halted his troops to make camp and rode to a tavern in Basking Ridge for a night's rest. In the morning he breakfasted and began to write a letter critical of Washington to General Horatio Gates.

"The ingenious maneouvre of Fort Washington has

unhinged the goodly fabrick we had been building," he wrote. "There never was so damned a stroke. Between us, a certain great man is most damnably deficient. . . ."

Just as Lee finished his letter, he heard a shout of alarm from his aide, Major James Wilkinson, who was standing at the window.

"Here, sir, are the British cavalry!" Wilkinson cried.

"Where?" yelled the astounded Lee.

"Around the house!" Wilkinson shouted.

A clatter of horses' hooves gave a chilling meaning to Wilkinson's words. Within seconds a troop of about thirty British dragoons under Colonel William Harcourt had surrounded the tavern.

General Lee jumped to his feet. "Where is the guard?" he cried. "Damn the guard, why don't they fire?"

The answer to that question was given by the flying feet of the general's vanishing guard trying to flee the dragoons who rode them down. General Lee was trapped. He glanced around him. A maid ran into the room to suggest that the general hide in a bed. Lee coldly refused. Outside, the voice of Colonel Harcourt became audible:

"If the general does not surrender in five minutes, I will set fire to the house."

There was not even time for General Charles Lee to clothe himself. In slippers, the collar of his blanket coat wide open, he went stiffly out the door to surrender.

Some of the dragoons hid their smiles. They knew their prisoner well.

Years ago the captured American general had been their commanding officer.

Even George Washington was shocked by the capture of General Lee. Like most of his countrymen, he overvalued the general's abilities, and he was sorry to lose him. Yet he had gained another 2,700 men with the arrival of Lee's troops, who were badly needed.

During that grim December when patriot fortunes were at their lowest, the commander in chief was once more engaged in the discouraging task of recruiting another army. By the end of the year most of the 6,000 men he commanded would be leaving, and few Americans were volunteering to take their place.

Nevertheless, in the midst of all these misfortunes—with the Middle states apparently moving into the enemy camp, with his army melting away, with Lee gone, and with criticism and blame heaped upon his head from every side—George Washington was planning to attack! He *had* to attack, he reasoned. There was no other way to rally the dying rebel cause. Even the barest gleam of the sun of victory had to shine upon his arms—or night would engulf the Revolution. Thinking thus, the commander in chief decided to cross the Delaware to strike the Hessians under Colonel von Donop.

Half this force was at Bordentown under Von Donop, and the other half in Trenton under Colonel Johann Rall, the hero of Fort Washington. It seemed to Washington that Rall was the more vulnerable of the two. So he decided to strike him. In order to implement the plan, Lieutenant Colonel John Cadwalader would cross the Delaware downriver opposite Bordentown to engage Von Donop and prevent him from sending reinforcements north to Rall. Meanwhile, Brigadier General James Ewing was to cross opposite Trenton with 900 men and block Rall's escape route south to Bordentown. Then Washington, leading the main body of about 2,400 men, would cross above Trenton on Christmas night and march downriver to launch a surprise attack before dawn.

On Christmas Day, all was in readiness. But with nightfall a howling snowstorm struck. Thick snowflakes lay melting on the boat cloak of General Washington, riding with his shivering troops toward McKonkey's Ferry. Nearing the ferry, the general was approached by Major James Wilkinson, the former aide of the captive General Lee. Wilkinson handed the general a letter from General Horatio Gates.

"By General Gates?" Washington asked, puzzled. It surprised him to learn that Gates, the northern commander based at Ticonderoga, might be in the area. "Where is he?" he asked Wilkinson.

"I left him this morning in Philadelphia."

"What was he doing *there?*"

"I understood him that he was on his way to Congress."

"On his way to *Congress*," Washington repeated, thunderstruck. Aware as he was that Gates, as well as Lee, had been sharply critical of him, the commander in chief could guess what Gates might be doing in Baltimore. More than one Congressman, outspoken in faulting Washington, would be willing to help Gates.

Courteously thanking Major Wilkinson for the letter, George Washington rode off toward the ferry. Now the attack could not fail.

Like most British and Hessian officers, Colonel Johann Rall, commanding at Trenton, had the utmost contempt for Americans. He did not believe they would dare attack him, and as a result he did not throw up defenses or send out regular scouting parties, as General Howe had ordered him to do. Even when he was warned that the Americans would attack him in the early morning of December 26—just as Washington planned—he believed that any strike against him would be a mere hit-and-run raid. A corporal's guard could rout those "country clowns," as he called the patriots.

Actually, it is doubtful if any kind of alarm could distract Colonel Rall from his customary revels. A fine fighter, he was also a heavy drinker. He believed that winter quarters were meant for wine and cards and little else. Drunk almost every night, he awoke each morning with a fearsome headache. The Hessian band and the guard waiting outside his window for the morning parade often had to stand shivering for hours in the cold until Colonel Rall finished his bath.

That was how Colonel Rall began Christmas Day, lying in his bath with his head aching while the troops

THE WORLD TURNED UPSIDE DOWN

and the bandsmen outside his window turned blue with cold. Then the parade was held, and both Colonel Rall and his men began to celebrate the nativity with gusto and full glasses. By nightfall almost all the Hessian soldiers were drunk, and Colonel Rall was nearly so as he sat at a table playing cards in the home of a wealthy Trenton Tory.

Just after dark, a messenger arrived with a note warning him that the American army was on the march. Colonel Rall stuffed it into his pocket unread. A little later he slipped from his chair, drunk, and had to be carried to his quarters.

The wind had risen, and the night had turned piercingly cold. A film of ice was already forming on the Delaware as Washington's men stood huddled by the ferry landing. They were under a rule of silence. No one was to break ranks under pain of death. In fact, "Victory or Death" was the watchword Washington had chosen for the assault.

Hunched over, their chins ducked into their collars against the snowflakes hurled in their faces by the wind, the Continentals began entering the boats brought up to the landing by John Glover's blue-coated Marbleheaders. For a time, ice cakes floating downriver threatened to damage, perhaps even overturn, some of the boats. Fortunately, however, the high wind blew at the backs of the Americans. At three o'clock in the morning the crossing was completed.

Now Washington separated his force into two divisions. One, under John Sullivan, was to march down the river road. The other, under Nathanael Greene, accompanied by Washington, would follow a parallel road two miles farther inland. Sullivan's division was to hit the lower end of Trenton; Greene's would come in at the top.

They moved out. Almost immediately, the men began to slip and fall. Ice had formed on the roads and made them treacherous. Sometimes the ice cut through the soldier's footwear and drew blood. Later that morning Major James Wilkinson was able to follow in their tracks by means of bloodstains in the snow. Just before eight o'clock in the morning of December 26, both divisions reached their destinations. Both encountered enemy pickets and attacked them.

"Der Feind! Heraus! Heraus!" the Hessian sentries cried. The enemy! Turn out! Turn out!

Stupefied from their Christmas revelry, the Hessian soldiers stumbled from their barracks. Lieutenant Jacob Piel ran to rouse Colonel Rall. Dressed in his nightgown, Rall poked his throbbing head out the window. Piel called to him. Stunned, Colonel Rall pulled on his uniform and rushed outside. To his dismay the Americans were emplacing artillery at the top of King and Queen streets. They had two guns to a street. Frantic, Rall put the scarlet-coated Lossberg Regiment on Queen Street, and on King Street to the left he formed

153

his own blue-coated regiment. To the rear, in reserve, were the black-suited Knyphausens.

At the top of King Street, Captain Alexander Hamilton called to his gunners. They blew on their slow matches and stuck them in the touchholes. The cannon bucked and roared. Grapeshot shrieked toward Rall's troops, cutting them down, driving them back. On Queen Street, the other cannon routed the Lossbergs. But the Hessians ran out their own cannon and fought back. Captain William Washington and Lieutenant James Monroe led an American charge. The Hessians fled, abandoning their cannon.

Now, below the town, Sullivan's division was attacking. Soon the men of Greene's division extended the unit's right flank to link up with Sullivan. If General Ewing's force held the escape bridge as they were supposed to be doing, the Hessians were trapped.

Ewing, however, had not crossed the river. Trenton's back door lay open, and hundreds of fleeing Hessians were already escaping through it. Nevertheless, Greene's and Sullivan's men still struck at the other Hessians.

"Use the bayonet!" General Washington cried. "I am determined to take Trenton."

Colonel Rall, however, was fighting back. He had begun to re-form his regiments to counterattack, when he was struck by two musket balls fired by American snipers. He fell from his horse, dying.

By then Sullivan's men had seized the bridge, and the three Hessian regiments surrendered. General Washington had taken Trenton. His men had captured 920 Hessians, killing about 25 more and wounding 90. American losses were incredibly light. Although two men had been frozen to death on the march to the battlefield, not a man had perished in combat, and only four were wounded.

The "country clowns," whom the dying Colonel Rall had despised so deeply, had conquered at last.

13

The "Old Fox" Slips Away

"This is a glorious day for our country," George Washington had exclaimed on the battlefield at Trenton, and it was indeed.

Eighteen months without a victory had at last been ended, and the patriots were elated. More, Trenton had finally exploded the myth of the terrible Hessian soldier, supposedly invincible in battle. Collecting his captives, Washington sent them across the river to Philadelphia, where they were publicly paraded so that the populace might see that the Hessians—the dreaded terrors of Long Island and Fort Washington—were just as weak as other men.

Shorn of their tall brass helmets and their bright bayonets, the captive soldiers were in truth a helpless lot, and for a few anxious moments, the cries and angry shouts of the Americans made the Hessians tremble in terror themselves. One Hessian soldier wrote: "The old women howled dreadfully, and wanted to throttle us all because we had come to America to rob them of their freedom."

Yet much as Trenton might lift American hearts while lowering British morale, General Washington was still in difficulty. By failing to cross the Delaware below Trenton, his other detachments had allowed many Hessians to escape and denied Washington vital reinforcements. With fewer than 2,400 men at his command, Washington at Trenton was in danger of being overwhelmed by the British forces which the shaken Sir William Howe had begun to pour into New Jersey. Moreover, his troops had captured a considerable amount of rum, and like the Hessians before them, the Americans were in danger of drinking themselves defenseless. So General Washington prudently ordered forty hogshead of rum stove in and retired across the river to Pennyslvania again.

There, he immediately began rebuilding his army, using the victory at Trenton as a lure for reenlistments. Many of his soldiers were so pleased by that triumph that they agreed to stay on for another six weeks, while a bounty of $10 induced others to sign up for another year. At the head of an army again, the audacious Washington recrossed the Delaware—seeking new victories with which to breathe new inspiration into the patriot cause.

Waiting for him was Lord Cornwallis, whose trip

home had been canceled by the indignant General Howe, and a large British army. Like his chief, Cornwallis was on fire for revenge, and he at once marched from Princeton to Trenton with about 5,500 men. Coming on the Americans in the late afternoon of January 2, 1777, the British drove in their pickets. Washington was left with his back to the Delaware. Aware of his plight, some British officers urged Cornwallis to finish him off before dark. But Cornwallis replied that his troops were too tired. He would rest them overnight and "bag the old fox" in the morning.

Washington called a council of war. His officers agreed that the situation seemed hopeless. At least where they were, the British had them in a box. Retreat was impossible. The Delaware was filling with blocks of ice, and the main road out of Trenton was blocked by enemy artillery. Retreat, however, was the last thing in General Washington's mind. Daring as ever, he proposed striking the enemy's rear. Behind Cornwallis lay Princeton, held by about 1,200 British—and behind Princeton was New Brunswick, unguarded and containing the British war chest of £70,000. Moreover, the side road to Princeton was open. Even though a thaw had turned the road into a muck of mud, it was agreed to follow it into the enemy's rear.

Fresh wood was thrown onto the campfires to delude the British into believing the Americans were bedding down for the night. A party of about 400 men was sent forward to work loudly with pick and shovel, as though digging fortifications. Then the weather took a lucky change for the colder. The road began to freeze. It was possible to take the wagons. Working rapidly, Washington's men wrapped the wagon wheels in rags to muffle them. Then, at one o'clock in the morning, marching under a rule of silence, leaving their campfires burning brightly, "the old fox" and his valiant little army slipped out of the bag held for them by Lord Cornwallis.

At Princeton that morning, Lieutenant Colonel Charles Mawhood led his brigade of 1,200 British regulars toward Trenton, where he was to join Cornwallis. Behind him he had left a garrison of 200 men holding Princeton. Riding over Stony Brook Bridge, Mawhood saw some rebels emerge from a wood to his left. He thought they were fugitives from Washington's "routed" army at Trenton. Actually, they were soldiers from General Hugh Mercer's advance guard. Behind them was Washington with the main body.

Nevertheless, Colonel Mawhood decided to take no chances. He pulled his brigade back over the bridge and led them on the double for the cover of an orchard. But the Americans beat him to it. They fortified a hedge and began raking the British. Calling for the bayonet, Mawhood charged and broke the American ranks.

Alarmed, General Mercer and Colonel John Haslet tried to rally the fleeing Americans. But the men ran around them. Mercer was bayoneted to death, and Haslet was shot through the head. At that General Washington came riding up the road on a big white horse. At once he saw that the situation was critical. The fleeing men could contaminate his entire army with terror. He tried to stop them. Waving his hat, he cried, "Parade with me, my brave fellows!" But they ignored him. Still determined, Washington galloped down the road to within thirty yards of Mawhood's redcoats. A British volley crashed out. A cloud of black smoke concealed Washington. One of his aides covered his eyes in horror. But when the smoke lifted, Washington was still there, waving his troops forward.

Fortunately, some of General Sullivan's troops had come down the road by that time. They ran forward toward Washington. Mercer's fragmented men were re-formed and returned to the fight, this time uttering battle cries. Now the British began to retreat down the road toward Trenton. Covered by a rear guard of dragoons, they made good their escape.

Princeton, meanwhile, had fallen to the rest of Sullivan's troops. Mawhood's garrison had taken refuge in Nassau Hall. Captain Alexander Hamilton ordered his gunners to bombard the building, and a single shot brought the British surrender.

Now the jubilant Washington turned his face eagerly toward New Brunswick. Here was his great chance. But then he realized how tired his men were. They simply could not march the eighteen miles to New Brunswick. The golden opportunity had passed. As Washington later wrote to Congress: "Six or seven hundred fresh troops, upon a forced march, would have destroyed all their stores and magazines" at New Brunswick, "taken . . . their military chest . . . and put an end to the war."

Deeply disappointed, Washington ordered his men to march to Morristown instead, and there he and his army went into winter quarters.

14

Defeat and Retreat

Since Bunker Hill, the British plan for reconquering the colonies had been based on the junction of two armies—one from Canada, another from New York City —on the Hudson River in the vicinity of Albany. In the spring of 1777, however, Sir William Howe changed this design. Instead of pushing up the Hudson to meet General Burgoyne's army driving down from Canada, he proposed to strike at the rebel capital in Philadelphia.

Even though the flood of loyalists into the British camp had been sharply slowed by the American victories at Trenton and Princeton, General Howe still believed he could crush the rebellion in the middle colonies. Strike at Philadelphia, draw Washington into a critical battle where he could be destroyed, and the American

Revolution would become a footnote in British history.

Not all of Howe's officers agreed with the plan. Some thought he should hold to the original strategy of a thrust at the back of New England. Others wondered if Washington would really fight for Philadelphia. They said that the rebels did not place the same value on a capital as Europeans did. Nevertheless, Howe stuck to his design. In July, after frittering away a month vainly trying to lure Washington into decisive battle in New Jersey, he put 14,000 men aboard transports and set sail for the mouth of the Delaware River.

En route, the skipper of a British frigate came aboard Howe's command ship to warn him of the dangers of navigating the Delaware.

Dismayed, Howe changed course, steering instead for the Chesapeake Bay. On August 14 he began landing troops at Head of Elk, Maryland. Although he was now only fifty miles away from his objective, Philadelphia, he had nevertheless allowed the fine campaigning months of May, June, July, and most of August to slip away. In that interval his opponent had had time to raise and train a new army.

Although George Washington had planned to stay in Morristown only a few days, he was compelled to stay there for nearly five months. There, "frozen in" by the raw cruel winter of northwest Jersey, he almost lost his army to the twin scourges of smallpox and hunger.

163

By March he had fewer than 3,000 men to command.

Nevertheless, he did not lose hope, and he once again was able to recruit enough replacements so that by spring his strength had risen to 9,000 men. Among his new soldiers were two notable recruits from Europe: the German Baron Johann de Kalb, a giant of a man and a veteran officer, and the French Marquis de Lafayette, a young and eager idealist. With the help of such officers Washington was able to improve the training of his men.

From France, then secretly assisting the colonies, came 22,000 muskets and hundreds of cannon. Thus, it was with a better trained and armed army that Washington moved to prevent Howe from capturing Philadelphia.

On September 11, 1777, he met him at Brandywine Creek.

The Brandywine lies roughly twelve miles above Head of Elk, where Howe had landed. In those days, it was passable by numerous fords, or shallow places where men and horses might wade the stream. Washington's plan was to guard the east bank of the Brandywine— that is, between Philadelphia and Howe's army—and to guard the fords. Thus, he put his left flank on Pyle's Ford, his center at Chad's, and his right at Painter's and Brinton's. Other crossings were watched by smaller forces. However, Trimble's Ford, seven miles north of Chad's, was left open. And Howe, of course, was marching on Trimble's.

164

As he had done at Long Island, Howe was trying to get into Washington's rear. Having ordered General Wilhelm von Knyphausen to hold the Americans "in place" at Chad's Ford—that is, to keep them occupied— he had taken Cornwallis and the main body north. Coming to Trimble's Ford, he had secretly crossed and swung south to come in behind the unsuspecting Americans.

Confident, advised that there was no enemy moving toward Trimble's, Washington thought that Von Knyphausen across the Brandywine at Chad's Ford was in fact the entire British army. But then, a bare-legged farmer named Thomas Cheyney was brought to his headquarters. Frantic, Cheney told Washington he had seen Howe cross the Brandywine. Some of Washington's staff officers sniffed at his story. They said Cheyney was probably a Tory, sent to deceive Washington.

Indignant, Cheyney shouted, "I'd have you know I have this day's work as much at heart as e'er a blood of ye!" Then he dropped to his knees to draw a map in the dust to show Washington exactly where the British were. Washington shook his head. Stung again, the farmer cried, "You're mistaken, General! My life for it you're mistaken. By hell, it's so! Put me under guard till you find out it's so."

Now Washington was torn by doubts—until a courier from General John Sullivan arrived with the message that the British were, in fact, in his right rear and marching down on him. Washington was stunned. It was Long Island all over again!

Reacting rapidly, the American commander ordered Sullivan to block the British at Birmingham Meeting House, about a mile to his right rear. Sullivan obeyed, taking position on a hill—only to be driven off by a British bayonet charge. Now, with Sullivan's entire left breaking and in danger of being swept away, Von Knyphausen began attacking the Americans at Chad's Ford. His men were forcing their way across the river. Washington's army was in danger of being caught between two forces. Even so, Washington realized that the main battle was at Birmingham Meeting House.

There the Americans fought valiantly. Five times they were driven from the hill, and five times they regained it. With them was the young Marquis de Lafayette, who had galloped north to the battle. Nevertheless, the British weight of men and metal seemed destined to carry the day—until General Nathanael Greene arrived with a relief column.

Opening their ranks to allow Sullivan's exhausted troops to pass through them to rest and re-form, Greene's men closed up again to halt the British onslaught. They held them. To the south, at Chad's Ford, Von Knyphausen's soldiers had forced a crossing of the Brandywine. But the Americans, led by "Mad" Anthony Wayne, were retiring in good order. With Howe halted and Von Knyphausen hesitating, darkness fell upon the battlefield at Brandywine. Under cover of the dark Washington withdrew to Chester and eventually to Germantown.

Once again Sir Willian Howe had outmaneuvered

George Washington. But once again he had failed to destroy him. Washington had saved his army.

Although the Americans had been defeated at the Battle of the Brandywine, their commander was still determined to prevent Howe from capturing Philadelphia. Marching and countermarching with the Schuylkill River at his back, Washington successfully held Howe at bay for two weeks. Many of the British officers were astonished by the "amateur" Washington's maneuvering skill and dismayed by the marching stamina of his "amateur" army. In the end, however, Howe feinted with his left to draw Washington away and then threw his army across the Schuylkill. On September 26, eight days after Congress had again abandoned Philadelphia, this time fleeing to York, Pennsylvania, Howe entered the American "capital." As he had expected, he received a hero's welcome. At last, it seemed, he had found the "true Americans." But then, to his astonishment, the "defeated" Washington attacked him.

In the fall of 1777 Washington and the men of his Continental Army should have been dejected. They had just been beaten by the British again and had lost Philadelphia, the national capital and the largest city in America. They had also been shaken by the Paoli Massacre, a surprise attack in which the British caught a unit of Americans silhouetted by the light of their campfires and had slaughtered them with the bayonet. Three hundred men were killed or wounded in that single swift action, and another hundred were captured.

Nevertheless, the Americans chose to forget this, dwelling instead on the new steadiness with which Washington's army marched and fought. To them the "capital" at Philadelphia was just another city—and a Tory stronghold at that. Finally, there had been great news from the north, where Gates' army had met and defeated Burgoyne's in the first Battle of Freeman's Farm. Thus, it was a buoyant, surprisingly confident army that Washington led against Howe on the night of October 3.

Coming against Howe with 9,000 regulars were 9,000 Continentals and about 3,000 militia. They were in four columns: militia on the right; then Sullivan's troops; then Greene's; then more militia. Sullivan and Greene in the center were the main striking force. The militia on the flanks were intended to strike at Howe's flanks and crumple them. On paper it was a pretty plan. On earth, however, where men march and fight, it was a bad one.

It was much too complicated. Even Howe's veterans commanded by Howe himself, a master tactician, would have had difficult in executing it. Worse, these four separate American columns were to make a night march of sixteen miles over four different roads and then come together at once in the dark to attack! And yet, involved as the scheme was, Washington nearly made it work.

Sullivan's force surprised the British light infantry. Troops under Mad Anthony Wayne drove them back. Astounded, Sir William Howe, the founder and former commander of this elite unit, leaped onto his horse and rode to the front to rally his former comrades-in-arms.

"For shame, light infantry!" he cried. "I never saw you retreat before. Form! Form! It's only a scouting party."

At that moment, a charge of grape exploded over Howe's head, and the dumfounded British commander realized that this was no "scouting party," but a major fighting force armed with artillery. Then Wayne's soldiers came dashing forward.

"Have at the bloodhounds!" they shouted. "Revenge the Paoli Massacre!"

Even Sir William Howe was borne backward by that rush, and Wayne's men began to take their revenge, slaughtering even soldiers who had thrown down their arms. British bugles sounded the retreat for the first time in the war. Jubilant, the Americans pursued.

But then a fog began to settle over Germantown. The clouds of battle smoke formed by the pungent black powder used in those days became even denser, and both sides lost sight of each other. Under cover of the smog, a company of British ran into the Chew House, a large stone mansion which lay directly in the American path. Colonel Henry Knox, with Washington's approval, tried to batter the house down with cannon shot. But he could not. After losing valuable time, Washington ordered his troops to push on.

Now the complication of the battle plan and the confusion that always reigns on the battlefield began to work against the Americans. First, Nathanael Greene with two-thirds of the American army had not yet appeared. Misled by a guide, Greene was an hour late, and when he did reach Germantown, one of his divisions blundered into Wayne's rear. Just then, Wayne heard the bombardment of the Chew House. Thinking it meant that the rest of Sullivan's troops were in trouble in his rear, he turned to help them—and ran into Greene's lost division.

Both American forces fired on each other and fled. This opened a gaping hole on Sullivan's left flank, and the re-formed British went charging into it. Now Sullivan gave way. His men broke and ran. So did the entire American army. Brokenhearted, Washington tried to halt them. They ran around him, some holding up empty cartridge boxes to show they were out of ammunition. It was not really their fault. General Wayne might complain, "We ran from victory," but the troops had actually fought bravely. It was the confusion of a complicated plan that undid the Americans at Germantown.

For the fifth time George Washington had dueled William Howe—and lost. Yet for the fifth time he had saved his army. Unshakable as ever, never taking counsel from his fears, Washington drew his army safely off and led it into the sanctuary of a place called Valley Forge.

15

Saratoga: The Turning Point

Before "Gentleman Johnny" Burgoyne set out for Canada in the spring of 1777, he bet his friend Charles James Fox, an influential Member of Parliament, a sum of $150 that he would be home victorious by Christmas.

That was how confident General Burgoyne was that he, rather than any other British commander, would have the honor of bringing the contemptible Americans to heel. When he arrived in Canada in May, he immediately began to prepare to put his own plan for victory into effect. This was merely to drive south to Albany while a second, smaller force under Lieutenant Colonel Barry St. Leger struck east from Oswego to Albany. Joined together, the entire British force would establish a linkup along the Hudson with General Sir Henry

Clinton, then in New York City with about 3,000 men.

Burgoyne's army totaled about 7,200 soldiers, all regulars, of whom about half were German mercenaries. He also had 400 Indians and about 250 Canadians. In June he led this force toward the Americans in Fort Ticonderoga.

Fortunately for Burgoyne, quarrels between Generals Schuyler and Gates had so weakened the patriot northern army that there were only 2,500 men holding Ticonderoga. Worse, Gates had neglected to fortify Sugar Loaf Hill to the southwest of the fort. Even after Benedict Arnold, still limping from the wound he had received at Quebec, managed to scramble up Sugar Loaf to disprove Gates' claim that the hill could not be climbed, the northern commander had stubbornly refused to change his mind. Thus, when Burgoyne and his Anglo-German army appeared outside the fort, they set to work putting artillery atop Sugar Loaf. When this was done and the Americans found themselves looking up into British muzzles, Fort Ticonderoga had to be abandoned.

Exulting, the British pursued the retreating Yankees. But they could not overtake them, and when the patriots reached the safety of Fort Edward, Burgoyne called a halt in Skenesboro. There he considered the alternatives of retracing his steps to Fort Ticonderoga, whence he could move easily over water to Fort Edward, or of moving overland from Skenesboro to the fort. Deciding that the patriots might mistake a "retrograde motion" to Ticonderoga as a British retreat, he chose the more diffi-

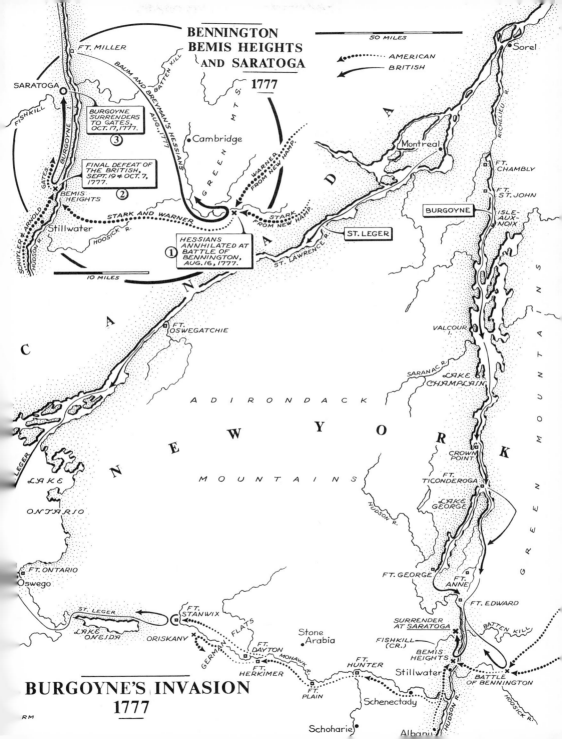

BENNINGTON
BEMIS HEIGHTS
AND SARATOGA
1777

50 MILES

← ▸▸▸▸ AMERICAN
← ─── BRITISH

FT. MILLER

SARATOGA

BAUM AND BREYMAN'S HESSIANS, AUG. 1777

BATTEN KILL

BURGOYNE SURRENDERS TO GATES, OCT. 17, 1777. ③

FISHKILL

BURGOYNE

Cambridge

GATES

FINAL DEFEAT OF THE BRITISH, SEPT. 19 & OCT. 7, 1777. ②

WARNER FROM NEW HAMP.

BEMIS HEIGHTS

SCHUYLER & ARNOLD

Stillwater

STARK AND WARNER

GREEN MTS.

STARK FROM NEW HAMP.

HOOSICK R.

HUDSON R.

HESSIANS ANNHILATED AT BATTLE OF BENNINGTON, AUG. 16, 1777. ①

10 MILES

Sorel

RICHELIEU R.

Montreal

FT. CHAMBLY

FT. ST. JOHN

BURGOYNE

ISLE-AUX-NOIX

ST. LAWRENCE R.

ST. LEGER

C A N A D A

FT. OSWEGATCHIE

VALCOUR I.

SARANAC R.

LAKE CHAMPLAIN

A D I R O N D A C K

CROWN POINT

FT. TICONDEROGA

N E W   Y O R K

M O U N T A I N S

LAKE GEORGE

LAKE ONTARIO

G R E E N   M O U N T A I N S

FT. ONTARIO

Oswego

LEGER

FT. GEORGE

FT. ANNE

FT. EDWARD

FT. STANWIX

ST. LEGER

LAKE ONEIDA

ORISKANY

GERMAN FLATS

FT. DAYTON

Stone Arabia

FT. HERKIMER

MOHAWK R.

FT. PLAIN

FT. HUNTER

SURRENDER AT SARATOGA

FISHKILL (CR.)

BEMIS HEIGHTS

Stillwater

BATTLE OF BENNINGTON

BATTEN KILL

HUDSON R.

HOOSICK R.

Schenectady

Schoharie

Albany

BURGOYNE'S INVASION
1777

RM

cult overland route. After all, he reasoned, the rebels "have no men of military science."

Perhaps, but they were certainly not lacking in energy. Even as Burgoyne moved out again, 1,000 Yankee axmen littered his path with huge felled trees "as plenty as lampposts upon a highway about London." They destroyed bridges and dug ditches from the bogs to create new swamps in the British path. Then, with the British toiling slowly through the wilderness, the Americans withdrew to Stillwater on the Hudson. On July 29, three weeks after he had reached Skenesboro, Burgoyne arrived at Fort Edward. It had taken him twenty-one days to advance twenty-three miles, of which eight had been over unobstructed water! In the interval, his intended victims had eluded him and left him an empty fort. Meanwhile, his men were exhausted, and his Indians were getting out of hand. The British had not been long at Fort Edward before a party of their Indians captured and murdered a local beauty named Jane McCrea.

With this, the countryside began to rise against Burgoyne.

Not only New York State but neighboring New England as well had become inflamed by the story of the murder of Jane McCrea. Moreover, New England realized that any success scored by Burgoyne in New York would mean that much more danger to their own back door. Thus it was that the New Hampshire General Court moved quickly to raise a brigade to "check the progress of Burgoyne."

John Stark, one of the heroes of Bunker Hill, was placed in command. Collecting about 1,500 men, Stark marched them to Manchester. There he received orders to join General Schuyler at Stillwater on the Hudson. Stark refused. He wanted nothing to do with the Continental Army or the Congress from which it took orders. Congress had repeatedly snubbed John Stark, promoting junior and untried colonels over his head. Unmoved by rebukes from his superiors, Stark marched his men south toward Bennington, leaving word for Colonel Seth Warner to join him there with the Green Mountain Boys.

Unknown to Stark, a foraging party of about 500 men—mostly dismounted dragoons from Brunswick, Germany—was also headed toward Bennington. They sought cattle for Burgoyne's hungry army and horses for the Brunswickers. Lieutenant Colonel Friedrich Baum, himself a Brunswicker, was in charge of the expedition. Nearing Bennington, Baum became alarmed by the number of Yankee irregulars hanging on his front and flanks, and he sent back to Burgoyne for reinforcements. About 650 soldiers under Lieutenant Colonel Heinrich von Breymann, another German, were ordered out to assist Baum. Before they could arrive, however, on August 15, a rainy day, Baum blundered into John Stark's brigade at Walloonsac River below Bennington.

At once Baum marched his men to high ground and began to dig in. The next day Stark prepared to attack. First, he gathered groups of militiamen and had them put the Tory white paper badges in their hats. In shirt sleeves, flaunting their badges, but still grasping their weapons, the men slouched forward. Thinking they were loyalists, Baum allowed them to infiltrate his front and rear. It was then that John Stark is supposed to have uttered his famous battle cry:

"There, my boys, are your enemies. You must beat them, or Molly Stark is a widow tonight."

With that there was a crash of patriot musketry—and Baum's Indians and Tories fled. Nevertheless, the other troops fought on. Baum's Brunswickers drew their swords and tried to cut their way to freedom. But the Americans drove them back. Baum himself was killed, while only 9 of his 374 Germans escaped death or capture. At noon, it appeared that the battle was over— until Von Breymann arrived with his reinforcements.

So, too, did Seth Warner with reinforcements for Stark, and between them the Americans struck at Von Breymann so furiously that the German commander was compelled to retreat. In all, both actions at the Battle of Bennington cost the Von Breymann-Baum forces more than 500 casualties, against 30 Americans killed and 40 wounded. More important, the victory was the first in a series of blows that were to shatter British morale.

A few days after Burgoyne had stopped to rest at Skenesboro, Barry St. Leger at Oswego on Lake Ontario began striking east toward Albany. There he intended to place himself and his mixed force of regulars, Tories, and Indians under Burgoyne's command. St. Leger's path, however, was blocked by about 750 patriots holding Fort Stanwix. On August 3, the British invested the fort.

News of the British advance from Oswego, together with reports of the murder of Jane McCrea, had already brought about 800 New York militia rallying to the call of General Nicholas Herkimer. Marching to relieve Stanwix, the Americans were ambushed at Oriskany, and Herkimer was killed. With this, St. Leger increased his pressure upon the American stronghold. Before he could capture it, however, one of its commanders, Lieutenant Colonel Marinus Willett, stole through the British lines to reach General Schuyler at Stillwater. Willett begged Schuyler for help, and to the consternation of many of his officers, who were against any "weakening" of the northern army, "the damned Dutchman" agreed to send 1,000 men to Stanwix.

As might be expected, Benedict Arnold was the only general at Stillwater willing to lead the expedition. As was not typical, this time Arnold decided to take the enemy by subtlety rather than storm. Seizing a dim-witted prisoner named Hon-Yost Schuyler, Arnold told the man's mother he would hang her son unless she persuaded him to do as Arnold asked. The woman agreed, and Hon-Yost was prevailed upon to go ahead of the Americans with an exaggerated report of their strength. Arnold had had the man's coat shot full of holes to verify his story of escape, and he also sent a friendly Oneida Indian after him to support Hon-Yost's report of a powerful American relief force.

When the two arrived in St. Leger's camp, one after

the other, their dovetailing stories frightened the British commander's Indian allies away. Then the loyalists fled, and there was nothing for St. Leger to do but to raise the siege of Fort Stanwix and return to Oswego.

Bennington had whittled Burgoyne's strength; Stanwix had denied him reinforcements.

When Sir William Howe turned south toward Pennsylvania, leaving Burgoyne, in effect, to fend for himself, General George Washington made the prophetic remark "Now let all New England turn out to crush Burgoyne." In truth, the American war chief might have said, "New England, and France," if only because French weapons were beginning to arrive in New England ports in a flood. Like the soldiers who fought the British at the Brandywine, the New Englanders hastening to Stillwater on the Hudson were armed with French muskets and cannon.

Meanwhile, the northern army based at Stillwater had had a change of command. Congress, seeking a scapegoat for the loss of Ticonderoga, had replaced Philip Schuyler with Horatio Gates. A cautious commander, Gates had decided to fight a defensive battle. On the advice of the Polish engineer Thaddeus Kosciusko, he chose a site on the west bank of the Hudson where a narrow pass between the river and the hills formed a bottleneck through which Burgoyne's army had to pass en route to Albany. In this defensive strategy, even though he did not please the bold Benedict Arnold, with whom he was already exchanging open dislike, Gates was probably correct. Burgoyne would have to attack, if only because he grew weaker by the day while Gates grew stronger.

The losses at Bennington, the failure of St. Leger to come to his aid, and the necessity of leaving a garrison at Ticonderoga had reduced Burgoyne's forces to about 5,000 men. Gates' strength meanwhile had increased to around 15,000 and was rising hourly. The longer Burgoyne waited, the more surely he would seal his doom, and so, on September 19, 1777, he attacked.

His objective was Freeman's Farm, a few miles south of Saratoga. The Americans had fortified the area, but a hill on the left flank had been left open. Burgoyne decided that if he could seize this high ground, he could command the patriot position just as he had done with Sugar Loaf Hill at Ticonderoga. So he ordered Baron Friedrich von Riedesel to hold down the American right along the Hudson while he himself drove at the American center at Freeman's Farm. Major General Simon Fraser, meanwhile, would sweep wide around the American left.

Unfortunately for Burgoyne, Benedict Arnold commanded on the American left. The moment the British attack began, Arnold asked Gates for permission to attack the British opposite Freeman's Farm. Gates hesitated. Arnold asked again, and Gates sent him Daniel Morgan's sharpshooters and Henry Dearborn's New Hampshire Regiment. With these additional troops, Arnold checked Fraser's thrust and began probing for the enemy soft spot.

Finding it between Fraser and Burgoyne, he threw fresh units into the battle and drove the British back. For a time the Americans held abandoned British artillery, until the redcoats recovered it with a bayonet charge. Nevertheless, American snipers in the trees began to scourge the British gunners, carefully picking off the officers. With enemy guns falling silent, Arnold thought he saw the chance to strike the knockout blow at the faltering British center. Appealing to Gates for more troops, he was refused. Later Gates changed his mind, but he sent the reinforcements to the left rather than to the center. With that, the golden moment that lasts so fleetingly on the field of battle disappeared—and Baron von Riedesel brought his Hessians marching up from the British left to save Burgoyne.

Yet the Battle of Freeman's Farm had been an American victory. Burgoyne had lost more men—between 500 and 600, against Gates' losses of 300—and he could afford to lose the less. Moreover, his morale had been shattered. Arnold's bold and slashing attacks had startled his officers. One of them wrote: ". . . the courage and obstinacy with which the Americans fought were the astonishment of every one, and we now become fully convinced they are not that contemptible enemy we had hitherto imagined them, incapable of standing a regular engagement, and that they would only fight behind strong and powerful works." So convinced, his numbers again reduced and continuing to dwindle, aware that he could expect little help from Sir Henry Clinton to the south, Burgoyne again attacked.

This second assault was a desperation swing, aimed again at the American left. This time, however, Horatio Gates was in command there. Because Gates' reports had ignored Arnold's leadership at Freeman's Farm, the flamboyant little soldier from Connecticut had angrily thrown up his commission, and Gates had relieved him of his command. Yet it was impossible for Arnold to leave a battlefield, and he had hung around the camp. Thus, it was Arnold who leaped upon a big brown horse to lead the charge that broke the British center and drove it back. The enemy, however, rallied—led by Simon Fraser. Realizing that the British could not afford to lose Fraser, Arnold asked Daniel Morgan to bring the enemy general down. Morgan in turn called upon a famous Indian fighter named Tim Murphy, and Murphy's third shot fired from a treetop mortally wounded Fraser.

With Fraser dying, the British faltered. Arnold prepared the knockout blow, only to be wounded himself— shot in the same leg that was hit at Quebec. With the Battle of Bemis Heights sputtering toward its close, Arnold was carried from the field on a stretcher. Burgoyne, meanwhile, had had enough of the Americans. Leaving 500 sick and wounded around him, he withdrew to the "sanctuary" of Saratoga.

There he and his officers fell into a deepening despair while Gates slowly drew a ring of steel around him. For the British there seemed no way out. The troops were exhausted scarecrows. Burgoyne had gone sixteen days without changing his clothes. There were bullet holes in his hat and waistcoat. Day after day the American artillery pounded his lines. On October 12, a cannonball nearly struck Burgoyne. On the following day he began negotiations for surrender.

And then, miraculously it seemed, there came news that Sir Henry Clinton to the south had burst through the patriot forts on the Hudson River. Relief might come any day! But it did not, and Burgoyne realized with sinking heart that Clinton did not have the strength to come to his rescue. Nevertheless, he delayed surrendering, so that Gates, fearing Clinton might come up behind him and trap him between two forces, became anxious to disarm Burgoyne. Thus, he changed his demand from unconditional surrender to a "Convention." Burgoyne's troops would be allowed to return to Great Britain under a promise not to serve again in America. Eventually, Congress repudiated the "Convention," and the British army which surrendered at Saratoga was moved from Boston to a prison camp in Virginia.

Major General John Burgoyne, of course, was permitted to return home on parole. Perhaps, as he took ship for England—the first general in history to surrender a British army to a so-called rabble in arms—he remembered what his friend Charles James Fox had said when he bet him that he would crush the colonies.

"Be not over hopeful in your expectations," Fox had warned him gently. "I believe when next you return to England you will be a prisoner on parole."

16

Enter the French

To all those separate actions which contributed to the undoing of Gentleman Johnny Burgoyne—to Ticonderoga, Bennington, Oriskany, Stanwix, Freeman's Farm, Bemis Heights, and Saratoga—history has given the single name of the Battle of Saratoga. And Saratoga was the most decisive conflict of the Revolution.

It proved to be the turning point of the war. By this great victory the patriot army inspired Congress to adopt the Articles of Confederation, by which the thirteen separate colonies were eventually to become the United States of America, Saratoga also brought France and then Spain into open support of the Americans and war with Britain. In February, 1778, France signed an alliance with the United States and later declared war on Britain. A year later Spain followed suit. Next came Holland, ordering its Dutch West Indies to increase their aid to the Americans. Finally, Catherine of Russia, from whom a once-friendly England had formerly sought troops, organized a League of Armed Neutrality with the objective of blocking British trade. In effect, the American Revolution had embroiled Britain in a world war with all its old enemies, as well as some of its former friends. And all this was due to Saratoga.

One unhappy effect of the victory, however, was that it gave encouragement to those critics of George Washington who were also friends of Horatio Gates. Carefully neglecting the name of Benedict Arnold in his reports, Gates had created for himself a halo of glory which seemed to emphasize the shame of Long Island, Fort Washington, Germantown, and the Brandywine. Such powerful Congressmen as Samuel and John Adams, as well as Richard Henry Lee, put themselves behind a movement by which Gates was made president of the revived Board of War. Technically, then, he became Washington's superior. Congress also named General Thomas Conway as inspector general, much to Washington's indignation. And it was Conway, an Irish-born officer of the French army, who gave his name to the so-called Conway Cabal.

This was the movement by which Washington's critics supposedly sought to replace him with Gates as commander in chief. Actually, they did not, and it is probable that Gates did not seek the position. However, it seemed that way at the time, chiefly because of the letters which Conway wrote belittling Washington and Gates' fondness for glory and the friendship of powerful Congressmen. In the end, Conway was wounded in a duel by an angry friend of Washington's, finally returning to France, and Gates discredited himself by proposing another invasion of Canada, which even Congress could see was foredoomed to bloody failure.

Nevertheless, the Conway Cabal dismayed and frustrated General Washington and many of his top officers, who were then, with the men of the Continental Army, passing through the dreadful ordeal of a winter at Valley Forge. There, in a cluster of hills about twenty miles from Philadelphia, Washington had taken his army. As he well knew, Valley Forge was far from the best place to send his army into winter quarters. It was not a good farming region, where food and forage might have been plentiful, and it was in Chester County, an area notoriously hostile to the patriot cause. Moreover, being so close to Philadelphia and the British, it was far from secure. Yet it was just because of this proximity that Washington chose Valley Forge. Being so close to the enemy would demonstrate to General Howe and America at large that there was still an American army in being that was unafraid of the British.

Still, the living conditions at Valley Forge turned out to be appalling. Although history has made much of the cold weather there, it was actually a mild winter. What made it unbearable was the selfish and cruel indifference of the American people. Soldiers at Valley Forge went half-naked because Boston merchants refused to sell clothing to the American government except at prices which brought them profits of from 1,000 to 1,800 percent. Soldiers went hungry because New York's wheat and flour went to New England or the British army and because Connecticut's farmers would not sell their cattle at the prices fixed by the state government. So the men of the Continental army starved and froze, their bodies reduced to bags of skin and bones by a diet of cornmeal cakes and water, their smoky huts so cold that many of these half-clad men preferred to sit up all night rather than fall asleep and perhaps freeze to death.

"Not one whole shirt to a brigade," Anthony Wayne reported from Valley Forge. "For God's sake if you can't give us anything else—give us linen that we may be enabled to rescue the poor worthy fellows from the vermin which are now devouring them." And again: "Some hundreds we thought prudent to deposit some six feet under ground who have died of a disorder produced by a want of clothing."

Even the horses sickened and died of a lack of fodder, some 1,500 of them perishing that winter. And before they could be buried or burned—in itself a major task— their rotting flesh magnified the general stench issuing from the unsanitary mess that was Valley Forge. Indeed, many of the blanket-clad officers at Valley Forge remarked that to be deprived of one's senses—especially the ability to smell—would be a distinct blessing in that hideous, howling, stinking encampment. One miserable young private wrote: "Poor food—hard lodging—Cold Weather—fatigue—Nasty Cloaths—nasty Cookery—

Vomit half my time—smoak'd out of my senses—the Devil's in it—I can't Endure it—Why are we sent here to starve and freeze . . . ?"

Meanwhile, all around them brilliant balls and masquerades were being held by the profiteering "patriot" merchants and war shirkers, who had become bloated, in effect, on the blood of the Continental Army.

This, too, embittered the Continentals. As one of them wrote: "I know of no reason why one part of the community should sacrifice their all for the good of it, while the rest are filling their coffers."

It was almost as though the civilian population of America believed that suffering and danger were the soldier's proper portion, while comfort and safety were the true lot of the civilian. In this they also reflected the American's deep distrust of the military. The country's leaders, notably such men as John Adams or Thomas Jefferson, seemed to see a potential dictator in every general's uniform. They talked endlessly of "freedom" but never came to the battlefields on which it was being won. Instead, Adams warned his countrymen to keep "a watchful eye on the army, to see that it does not ravish from them that liberty for which all have been contending." *All have been contending.* Contending where? At Baltimore, York, Annapolis, or any of the other snuggeries to which Congress rushed whenever a redcoat came within thirty miles of Philadelphia?

Suspicious of the soldiers who were saving them, the politicians even refused their appeals for the barest necessity. Thus, when officers of the Pennsylvania Line at Valley Forge requested clothing, the state's council turned them down lest they try to lord it over civilians and strut about in "Fine beaver Hats, Gold Laced Hats, Silken Stockings, fine Cambrick and other expensive Articles of Dress." In truth, it was the politicians who were dressed in silks and furs and gold while the soldiers wore rags and tatters.

Most wondrous of all, despite such selfish indifference to its travail, the Continental Army not only refused to fall apart but actually tightened its discipline. Valley Forge became not the coffin of the Continental Army, but its cradle. The men who survived that cruel ordeal, said one Continental officer, were "the most virtuous men living" as well as "brave, patient soldiers." They were willing to suffer and even die for the cause in which they believed so devoutly. And this was the quality in the Continentals that impressed the "Baron" Friedrich von Steuben when he came to Valley Forge to train them.

Congress had appointed Von Steuben adjutant general of the Continental Army. The delegates had been impressed by his title, his "rank" of lieutenant general, and his close "friendship" with King Frederick the Great of Prussia. Actually, Von Steuben was not a baron or a general or a comrade of the great military master of Europe. Yet for all his pretensions, he was a very able soldier.

Other professional officers might have been shocked by the appearance of the ragged Continentals, but Von

Steuben saw only their sturdiness. This, he knew, this ability to withstand adversity, was the highest of soldierly virtues. What they needed now, he realized, was discipline and drill. Even here he wisely refrained from giving them Prussian drill. As he said himself, in the Prussian army an officer said to a soldier, " 'Do this,' and he does it, but I . . . I am obliged to say 'This is the reason why you ought to do that,' and then he does it."

Momentarily handicapped by his broken English, Von Steuben soon learned the rough language of the drill field, which he mixed with impeccable French. Sometimes, when he lost his temper with a particularly slow unit, he would shout at them in this mixture of pure French and foul English, and they would collapse with laughter. Eventually, because of his own good humor, Von Steuben gained the confidence of the Continentals. Before the spring of 1778 arrived, and with it fair weather for fighting, Von Steuben had given George Washington a disciplined army.

Washington's old rival, Sir William Howe, had gone home to England. Convinced that the Americans had only just begun to fight, Howe had asked Lord George Germain to relieve him of "this very painful service." On May 24, having advised the loyalists of America to throw themselves on the mercy of the patriots, Howe sailed down the Delaware for the last time.

Sir Henry Clinton was now in command, and this cold and gloomy general took charge with a sinking heart. He realized that to desert the loyalists as Howe had done was, in effect, to give up the fight. If the majority of "good" Americans were to be abandoned, how was the minority of "bad" Americans to be subdued? Next, Clinton feared for his army.

He knew that a large French fleet under Admiral Comte Charles d'Estaing was headed for America. The French could very well blockade the British fleet in the Delaware and nail Clinton's troops between themselves and Washington in New Jersey. Thus, when Clinton received orders to evacuate Philadelphia and sail for New York City, he decided instead to send only part of his forces by water. To load them all aboard ship might waste valuable time and give D'Estaing the chance to seal off the river mouth. So he put 3,000 downhearted Tories and two Hessian regiments aboard the ships, while crossing the Delaware himself with his main body to march overland across New Jersey.

Besides about 9,000 troops, Clinton had an enormous baggage train, filled for the most part with possessions of the Tories and merchants who had fled Philadelphia. Because of this, British progress was slowed to the extent that it took seven days to go forty miles. Even so, Clinton kept marching toward Sandy Hook, where he intended to meet the British fleet and take ship the remaining few miles.

On June 27, with his units strung out for almost a dozen miles, Clinton stopped to rest for the night at Monmouth Courthouse. There, aware of his enemy's vulnerable rear guard, Washington moved to attack him.

* * *

General Charles Lee commanded Washington's striking force. General Lee had been returned to the patriots in a massive exchange of prisoners of war. He was received with jubilation. Washington held a special parade in his honor and sat down to dinner with him at his headquarters in the presence of Mrs. Washington. Like almost all of his officers, the American war chief still regarded Lee as a "martial genius."

Unknown to any of them, however, Charles Lee had had a complete change of heart. While a captive of the British army, he had decided that the British were the world's best warriors and that the Americans, especially when commanded by the inept Washington, had no chance against British regulars. Worse, Lee had even changed his mind about the Revolution. In the presence of British officers, with whom he had passed a gay captivity, he had openly deplored it. He now believed that the British Empire should not be divided and that it should be ruled from London. So completely had Lee changed sides that he even drew up a plan of conquest for the Howe brothers.

None of the Americans suspected Lee's turnabout. Actually, it is doubtful if the returned general planned to betray his former comrades. But he did wish to bring peace between the rebels and the mother country. For this reason, he was always against a general engagement. Thus, when Washington offered him command of the force that would strike Clinton, he at first refused it. Then, seeing the honor go to the youthful Lafayette, he changed his mind and asked to be put in charge. Wash-

191

ington, always the gentleman, politely restored him to command.

June 28, 1778, was an unbearably hot and humid day, one of those days that are the special torment of the brutal New Jersey summer. In that moist and breathless heat, Sir Henry Clinton led most of his army toward Sandy Hook again. Behind him, guarding that slow-moving baggage train, he left a detachment of about 2,000 men.

It was here Washington ordered Lee to strike, hoping to capture Clinton's baggage. With no fixed plan of his own, Lee moved out at the head of 5,000 men. Soon his units became fragmented and disorganized. Individual skirmishes with the British rear guard began. Hearing them, Clinton wheeled and came hurrying to the rescue with the main body—and it was at this point that General Lee gave the order to retreat.

Soon the retreating Americans were running again. The British, remembering the patriot fear of bayonets, cheered and charged. And then, to the consternation of their officers, the redcoats began to fall. In that stifling heat, clad in their thick, stiff uniforms and weighed down with gear, just to run was to risk death. One grenadier became so thirsty he put his face into a pool of water, drank—and burst his insides. Two others went mad. Soon, the road was strewn with collapsed redcoats, of whom sixty actually died.

Nevertheless, news of the American retreat infuriated George Washington. His iron self-control snapped.

White with fury, he mounted the big white horse given to him that day by Governor Livingston of New Jersey and galloped off for the front. Those who saw him confront Lee never forgot the sight. A French officer said: "I saw for the first time what fury was, because anything more appallingly terrible than the face of General Washington when he appeared on the scene and galloped toward Lee I have never seen, nor has any one else. It was like the God of Battles intent to kill or destroy." One other witness wrote: " 'You're a coward' he cried to Lee in a thunderous voice, and then fired away a volley of oaths such as neither I nor any other human being ever heard before."

Ordering the crestfallen Lee to the rear, Washington stopped the retreat. He rode among the American units, encouraging them, re-forming them, meanwhile bringing up his main body. Aware that Clinton would attack him, actually hopeful of it, Washington went on the defensive. He chose high ground just west of a ravine. There he placed Stirling on the left, himself in the center, and Greene on the right. Wayne was given an outpost in Washington's front.

Their blood still up, the British charged, first striking Stirling on the left. There, in that dreadful heat, men fought for an hour. There also an artillery duel began, and the wife of a sergeant named Mary Hays made herself famous as "Molly Pitcher" by bringing water to the gunners. When her husband was wounded, she took his place on his gun. And it was here, on the left, that Washington was at last able to maneuver like a European general. Marching smartly under fire, American regiments were wheeled into line, and when they got around the British right flank, they saved Stirling's position.

Next, Clinton struck at Greene on the right. Lord Cornwallis personally led the assault. But he, too, was repulsed.

In front of Washington, Wayne's troops were under attack. "Steady, steady," Wayne cried to his men. "Wait for the word, then pick out the king-birds." At forty yards, the Americans crashed out a volley so terrible that it killed the British leader and broke the attack. Eventually, however, the British outflanked Wayne, forcing him to pull back. And at that point, the Battle of Monmouth came sputtering to an exhausted end.

Both sides lay gasping in the heat, waiting for the cool of night. At midnight Clinton arose and led his army safely away. By having saved his rear guard and baggage train, he might have rightfully been considered the victor. Actually, Monmouth was a draw. Both sides suffered about 350 casualties, half of them due to fatigue and heat exhaustion, and no important or vital ground was either won or lost.

For the Americans, however, Monmouth could be counted a "moral victory." The patriots had fought the British regulars to a standstill, and for the first time, under the proud, fatherly eye of Von Steuben, they had marched and maneuvered like professionals. More, Monmouth had rid George Washington of the last of his critics.

Demanding a court-martial, General Lee was dumfounded to find himself convicted of disobedience and sentenced to a year's suspension. "O that I were a dog," he cried bitterly, "that I might not call man my brother."

Thus, the Battle of Monmouth was another turning point. It left Washington in full command of a professional army, and it was also the last time either army met each other in pitched battle. After Monmouth, the purely American phase of the War of the Revolution came to an end. Thereafter, the new American flag— "Thirteen stripes alternate red and white, [with] thirteen stars white on a blue field"—was to flutter side by side with the golden lilies of France.

17

More Setbacks

With France as an ally and with a French fleet and soldiers sailing to his side, it was not too much for George Washington to hope that 1778 would be the year in which the knockout blow would be dealt the British.

Unfortunately, the year that had been begun so brilliantly at Monmouth began to turn dull with the tarnish of military setbacks in the West and missed opportunities in the East.

In the West, British-led Indians had taken to the warpath and begun to massacre American settlers. On the Fourth of July—deliberately mocking Independence Day—Colonel John Butler invaded the Wyoming Valley in Pennsylvania, where his red men tortured and killed hundreds of Americans. Men were burned at the stake or pressed alive on beds of burning coals, held there with pitchforks while their horrified families witnessed their agony. Others were placed in a circle while a half-breed squaw named Queen Esther went leaping and chanting around them, chopping off their heads. Even though the Indians eventually brought death and destruction to the entire frontier, Washington was unable to send rescue forces west. All that he possessed was needed in the East, where it was hoped that the French fleet under Admiral Comte d'Estaing would help defeat the British.

But D'Estaing arrived off the Delaware ten days too late to cut off Lord Howe's fleet, which had escaped to New York City. Next, Howe turned around to ferry Clinton's army safely across the Lower Harbor into Manhattan. Nevertheless, D'Estaing still could break into New York Harbor to destroy Howe's fleet, which was only half as large as his. Instead, he waited ten days outside the harbor bar, cautiously taking depth soundings there. Then, with the water a full thirty feet over the bar, he decided it was still not deep enough for his ships and sailed away.

"The wind could not have been more favorable for such a design," a relieved British officer wrote. "The spring tides were at the highest. We consequently expected the hottest day ever fought between the two nations."

So had George Washington, and the American commander was deeply disappointed. Still seeking a victory in 1778, Washington turned toward Newport, Rhode Island. Some 10,000 men under General John Sullivan, assisted by D'Estaing's fleet and 4,000 French soldiers, were to take this vital seaport from the British. However, the Franco-American force very quickly experienced the problems which vex coalition warfare. When allies combine to fight and do not speak the same language or fight the same style of battle, there is always misunderstanding and disagreement.

This happened at Newport. The fact that Sullivan put his troops ashore at Newport town first without waiting for the French to disembark annoyed the French officers. Then the Americans became enraged when the French fleet sailed out of the harbor to do battle with the British fleet on the high seas. This left Sullivan without the support he needed to storm the town. Meanwhile, on the night of August 11 a violent storm sprang up to scatter both the French and British fleets. After Admiral Lord Howe returned to New York and Admiral Comte d'Estaing took safety in Boston, it was decided to abandon the Rhode Island expedition.

But the echoes of that unhappy operation continued to crash around the ears of General Washington. On the one hand, the Americans, led by General Sullivan, taunted the French as "Heroes of Flight," and Sullivan publicly sneered: "If this is Gallic faith, we have formed a sweet and hopeful alliance." Next, two French officers were badly injured in Boston when they attempted to stop a riot between French and American sailors. For a time, it appeared that the new alliance would be strained past the breaking point, especially after D'Estaing sailed away for Martinique in November. However, Washington's strict prohibition of anti-French words and deeds among his officers and men, plus the natural charm of the French, eventually smoothed things over.

Nevertheless, the British still held New York City and Newport. In December they also gained a foothold in the South, when Savannah, Georgia, fell to a force of 3,500 regulars and Tories under Lieutenant Colonel Archibald Campbell. In the meantime, the western frontier had been tormented by tomahawk and firebrand once more. This time, the target was the patriot settlement at Cherry Valley in upstate New York, and the tormentor was Walter "Hellhound" Butler, the bloodthirsty son of Sir John Butler.

Thus, with the frontier ravaged, with New York and Rhode Island still in British hands and the enemy beginning to expand his foothold in the South, the campaign of 1778 came to a gloomy close. Stationing his army in a chain of posts beginning in Middletown, New Jersey, and extending to West Point and Fishkill in New York, and Danbury, Connecticut, Washington went into winter quarters.

18

"I Have Just Begun to Fight"

Although it seemed that the first fruits of the Franco-American alliance had been soured by defeat and dissension, the fact was that there had been solid, though unseen, advantages.

First, the mere presence of a powerful French fleet in American waters ended British sea supremacy there. They could no longer use their navy as they pleased. This, of course, is the value of a "fleet in being." By its mere presence, by its actuality, it compels the enemy to use some part of his strength—if only to watch this "fleet in being."

Also, the departure of Admiral d'Estaing for American waters convinced the British cabinet that it must evacuate Philadelphia, lest the French fleet trap it there. And after the British withdrew to New York City, the presence of the French fleet outside the harbor raised the specter of possible starvation. If D'Estaing could have successfully blockaded New York, he would have cut off Clinton's army from supplies at home.

All these benefits, though not immediately apparent, sprang from the single fact that the British position in America depended on sea power. If command of the sea was to be torn from their grasp, they had no hope of conquering the colonies. They would not be able to move their troops up and down the coast at will, and the long supply line on which they depended would be cut.

Thus, in June, 1779, when Spain declared war on Britain, Sir Henry Clinton's position in America became even more perilous. The combined navies of France and Spain were now arrayed against Britain. For the first time since the defeat of the Spanish Armada in 1588, Britain itself was in danger of being invaded. Moreover, D'Estaing was busy in the West Indies, taking island after island from Britain. As a result, Sir Henry Clinton was forced to limit his operations in America and to send 8,000 regulars from New York to the West Indies.

At one point, Clinton was so alarmed that he even considered evacuating New York City. He actually did abandon Newport. The port and town which had been the Franco-American objective of the preceding year was given up without a shot. And even though the huge fleet assembled to invade England eventually sailed home again without setting a man ashore on British soil, the mere fact of its presence had forced the British navy to recall many of its warships from America. As a result of this, American ports were opened to a swarm of privateers.

A privateer is an armed ship which, though owned privately, is authorized by government to make war on enemy shipping. A privateer keeps all the ships it captures, dividing the spoils among owner, captain, and crew. In this way, a poor government such as the United States avoided the high costs of building a huge navy on its own to attack Britain on the seas.

At first, American privateers were very successful, so much so that they seemed to grow richer waging war for profit than they had in peaceful commerce. Gradually, however, the entry of British privateers into the war reduced the American advantage. Then the British navy bottled up the tiny American navy in home ports—until the threat of a Franco-Spanish invasion forced Britain to recall her warships. With this, John Paul Jones entered American history.

Born just John Paul, "Jones" had gone to sea as a boy. Rising to captain, he was charged with murder in the West Indies, and although he proved his innocence, he was charged again with cruelty to his crew. At this point he changed his name to John Paul Jones and came to live in America.

Jones was an ardent son of liberty and joined the Revolution at the outset. He was one of the captains who responded when Benjamin Franklin, angered by British atrocities in America, called for revenge on British soil. In 1778, in command of the *Ranger*, Jones struck at the

British town of Whitehaven and burned vessels in port there. Thereafter, he scourged the shores of Britain, growing in strength, until, in September, 1779, he was able to put out from France at the head of four ships.

These were the brigantine *Vengeance*, 12 guns; the 32-gun frigates, *Alliance* and *Pallas*; and Jones' own flagship, *Bonhomme Richard*, 42 guns. At dusk of September 23, a British convoy was sighted. Guarding the merchantmen were *Serapis*, 50 guns, and *Countess of Scarborough*, 20. At once Jones signaled the attack. *Pallas* went after *Countess of Scarborough*, eventually subduing her, but for some unknown reason, both *Alliance* and the smaller *Vengeance* stood away from the battle. Jones in *Bonhomme Richard* was left to fight *Serapis* alone.

Jones' first broadside almost finished him. Two of three guns on *Richard*'s engaged side blew up, killing the crews and bursting the deck above them, and the third had to be abandoned. Still, Jones fought on, putting *Bonhomme Richard* alongside *Serapis* and lashing both ships together. For two and a half hours, in the pale light of the moon, the two ships lay together like boxers slugging toe to toe.

Slowly, mercilessly, *Serapis* began taking *Richard* apart. She sent her rotten timbers flying, shot holes in her hull below the waterline, and knocked out every American gun until only three were left. With his ship afire, listing and leaking, his pumps failing, Jones still fought on. When one of his gunners called to the *Serapis* for quarter, Jones broke his skull with his pistol. When the captain of the *Serapis* shouted to see if *Richard* really was striking her colors, Jones bellowed back, "I have just begun to fight."

In truth, that historic reply was no mere playacting. Jones knew that French marines in his fighting tops were taking a steady toll of enemy seamen. Once they had cleared the British rigging, they poured a scourging fire into her upper decks, thickening it with grenades and combustibles. Then a grenade tossed into a pile of cartridges set off an explosion that shook *Serapis* from stem to stern. Shortly afterward, *Alliance* entered the battle, and although some of her shots struck *Richard*, she put enough shells on *Serapis* to compel her to surrender.

Thus, the first sea fight of any size between the Americans and the British had resulted in an American victory. Even though John Paul Jones was forced to abandon the sinking *Bonhomme Richard* and transfer to *Serapis*, he had humbled the mighty British navy. And even though the British were eventually able to drive American privateers from the seas, this single great victory was to stand as the battle birth of the United States Navy.

19

Fizzle and Failure in '79

During the year 1779, the War of the Revolution slowed down as the rival forces, like boxers in the ring, sparred and probed while catching their breath for the fiercer fighting that lay ahead.

From the British standpoint, a slowdown was a necessity. Britain's war with France and Spain had compelled it to withdraw two-thirds of its ships from American waters. It had also caused it to weaken Sir Henry Clinton's army by some 14,000 soldiers. With so many of his men engaged elsewhere, Clinton could not afford the decisive battle with General Washington which Lord George Germain was forever demanding.

Thus, the campaigns of 1779 were for the most part hardly more than raids and skirmishes. The first of these was on the western frontier, in the so-called Illinois country. There, the previous year, the daring patriot leader George Rogers Clark had captured British outposts at Kaskaskia and Vincennes. But then Vincennes had been recaptured by Colonel Henry Hamilton, a British commander who was known as "the hair-buyer" for his policy of paying Indians for patriot scalps.

Determined to retake this important outpost, George Rogers Clark began marching from Kaskaskia, 150 miles to the southeast, at the head of 130 patriots and Frenchmen. It was early February, 1779, and the ice-cold rains and floods made the "march" a shivering, chattering, freezing nightmare in which canoes turned out to be as valuable as shoes.

At last Clark's valiant little band appeared before Vincennes. There Clark paraded his men back and forth to give the appearance of ten times their strength, and this ruse frightened Colonel Hamilton's Indian allies away. Then Clark settled down to a sniper war, ordering his sharpshooters to pick off the fort's defenders. His slender forces whittled, hoping to stall for time, Colonel Hamilton asked for talks. Clark was not deceived. Instead of consenting, he had five Indians who had been captured with scalps in their possession led out in full view of the fort, where they were tomahawked to death. Hamilton surrendered Vincennes.

With this successful expedition, George Rogers Clark had been able to deal a blow to British power in the Northwest. Nevertheless, because Fort Detroit remained in enemy hands, British-led Indian bands were still able to ravage the frontier.

In the West, meanwhile, General Washington moved to check the Indians who had carried out the massacres in the Wyoming and Cherry valleys the previous year. General Sullivan with 5,000 troops struck savagely at the Iroquois, destroying no less than forty of their towns. Yet, just because this expedition was a hit-and-run rather than a hit-and-hold operation, the British and their Indian allies became active in the area again as soon as the patriots withdrew. Throughout the war, the West and Northwest frontiers would be alight with the flames of Indian warfare. Meanwhile, the British regulars themselves had begun to make raids of their own, which, for sheer savagery, would make even an Iroquois blush.

The bloody raids which dishonored British arms in the summer of 1779 were the result of Lord North's last desperate attempt to bring "peace" to America. Surprised by the fierceness of American resistance, fearful of French entry into the war, Lord North had in early 1778 obtained Parliament's approval of his Conciliatory Proposals.

Under these, Britain would have agreed not to quarter troops in the colonies in time of peace, to make no changes in colonial charters, and to accept colonial representation in Parliament or else recognize the American Congress. If offered in 1774, these proposals would certainly have prevented the war. But by the time Lord Carlisle's commission arrived with them in America—in June, 1778—they were too little and too late.

Congress refused to talk to the Carlisle Commission.

Desperate, Lord Carlisle foolishly tried to bribe such American leaders as Benjamin Franklin and George Washington. Failing there, he just as unwisely appealed over the head of Congress to "the American people." Finding himself not only rebuffed but despised, Carlisle then proceeded to issue a proclamation threatening "a war of extermination" in America.

With this, frightful raids were mounted against the Connecticut towns of Fairfield, Norwalk, and New Haven. Redcoats were accused of "murdering old men, ravishing women and little girls, burning houses with the inhabitants in them, burning barns with the grain . . . cutting down all fruit trees, &c. &c." Even loyalist women were attacked by the British, who were delighted to bring their boring confinement in New York City to an end. Some of the prettier girls were actually carried away as prizes.

In his new headquarters at West Point, George Washington became so enraged by enemy atrocities that he urged Congress to authorize raids on English towns. Meanwhile, aware that another purpose of the British raids was to draw him out of West Point, he refused to budge. Instead, he ordered Mad Anthony Wayne to recapture Stony Point on the Hudson.

General Wayne commanded the American light infantry, an elite force of about 1,200 soldiers trained along the lines of Sir William Howe's light infantry. To retake Stony Point on the Hudson, Wayne proposed a night march and a surprise attack with the bayonet only.

On the night of July 15, his men moved out. They took into custody all the inhabitants of the area and also killed all the dogs along the line of march lest their barking betray them. Stealing softly along the riverbank, wading in two feet of water, they came to the fort. There they divided into three columns and started forward.

On the right, British sentries sighted Wayne's column and opened fire. An enemy ball grazed Wayne's head, knocking him down. Scrambling to his knee, the American commander urged his men forward, and they attacked, yelling and with outthrust bayonets.

In a brisk, bloody fight, the Americans subdued the fort. They lost 15 men killed and 83 wounded, against casualties of 63 killed, about 70 wounded, and 543 captured. But Stony Point, brilliant little victory that it was, was also only a hit-and-run raid. Eventually, Washington abandoned the fort. So, too, did Sir Henry Clinton, evacuating Verplanck's Point as well.

For the War of the Revolution had gone South for good, and Clinton needed men to help hold Savannah against the French.

When Washington learned that the Comte d'Estaing was returning with his fleet to American shores, he immediately made plans for an attack on New York City. Sea superiority, Washington believed, would enable him to trap Clinton's army and perhaps end the war. D'Estaing, however, had different ideas. With customary indifference to the wishes of the American commander, he had steered for Savannah instead.

On September 12 he put about 3,500 French soldiers ashore south of the town. A few days later he was joined by Count Casimir Pulaski with 200 horsemen and General Benjamin Lincoln with 1,350 Continentals and militia. Outnumbering the British about 5,000 to 2,400, D'Estaing did not storm the city, as he might easily have done. Instead, he summoned it to surrender, and in the name of the King of France. This immediately provoked General Lincoln, who insisted that any surrender must be to the Continental Congress.

To General Augustine Prevost commanding the mostly Tory force in Savannah, the summons was a heaven-sent opportunity. Pretending to take it seriously, he asked for a truce. After it was granted, he used the respite to strengthen his fortification and await reinforcements. They came—some 800 precious regulars—led by Lieutenant Colonel Maitland and arriving under cover of a fog. Then, to General Prevost's further delight, D'Estaing again delayed, deciding to take Savannah by siege tactics.

After he had begun to dig trenches toward the city and to bring big naval guns ashore, D'Estaing changed his mind once more. News that a British fleet was en route from the West Indies to Savannah made him decide to attack.

D'Estaing's plan of battle called for three columns. One was to march to the British right rear and try to force an entrance through the Sailor's Gate. Another was to make a feint at the British left, and the third, the main

210

blow, was to strike the British right on the Spring Hill Redoubt. Unfortunately, Sergeant Major James Curry, a deserter from the Charleston Grenadiers, informed Prevost of D'Estaing's plans. Thus, the British were ready and waiting when the Franco-Americans struck early in the morning of October 9.

Once the column moving toward the Sailor's Gate emerged from a swamp, British fire drove it back. Next, the second column made its feint at the British left. Prevost ignored it, calmly waiting for the main thrust at the reinforced Spring Hill Redoubt. When it came, a hail of British fire cut the Franco-Americans down. Still, the South Carolina Continentals led by Lieutenant Colonel Francis Marion—the legendary "Swamp Fox"—came charging all the way to the redoubt's parapet. Two officers attempting to raise a flag were shot down. So was Sergeant Jaspar, killed trying to duplicate his brave feat at Fort Moultrie.

At this point, with the Franco-Americans disorganized outside the redoubt, Colonel Maitland charged out in a British counterattack. Stubbornly standing their ground, the patriots and their French allies fought hand to hand for an hour. On their left, Count Pulaski tried to relieve the pressure on them by leading a cavalry charge. But British firepower tumbled his horsemen in the mud, and Pulaski was killed. With that, the allies fell back.

Savannah had held. Suffering about 150 casualties themselves, the British had inflicted a total of 850 on the Franco-Americans. That was enough for the Comte

211

d'Estaing. Rebuffing all of General Lincoln's pleas to renew the siege, he put his troops back aboard his ships and sailed away.

The fact that the French had failed a second time came as a deep shock to General Washington and his Continentals, beginning their second winter in Morristown. Washington's fears that the British would drive a deep wedge into the South, perhaps cutting off the entire region from the North, seemed to have been confirmed. Worse, the entire country was starving for good news, and now it would be compelled to pass the winter with its spirit nourished by tales of disaster.

That winter was probably the cruelest of the war. It was so cold that New York Harbor froze. Screaming blizzards buried Morristown in deep drifts of snow, blowing away the soldiers' tents or knocking down their makeshift shanties. Not even Valley Forge could compare to that second winter at Morristown. "We have never experienced a like extremity at any period of the war," Washington wrote. There was so little food that at one point Washington observed, "We have not at this day one ounce of meat, fresh or salt, in the magazine."

With great reluctance, Washington commandeered supplies from the surrounding countryside. As he expected, the people hated him for it. They did not feel obligated to feed the Continental Army, and yet, if that army starved, the Revolution would also die. The situation was a dreadful dilemma which Alexander Hamilton summarized with the remark "We begin to hate the country for its neglect of us. The country begin to hate us for our oppressions of them."

Runaway inflation was at the heart of the problem. Congress was powerless to stop it. A shortage of goods caused by the British blockade was made more serious by the demands of the armed forces. When greedy merchants and speculators kept raising the costs of goods, or else "cornered" certain products so that they could control the sale of them and thus charge what they pleased, prices climbed out of sight. Even the British could not have found a better way to ruin the American war effort, and George Washington so hated these selfish wreckers of the economy that he vowed he would like to hang all he could get his hands on.

Unfortunately, there was no way that Congress could prevent the profiteers from taking the enormous profits that sent prices soaring. In war, a democracy is always at a disadvantage, unless it suspends the freedom for which it is fighting. A dictator could always put such robber merchants in jail without bothering about whether or not their "rights" were being violated. This the lawmakers of a free people would not do, without turning dictator and bringing an end to liberty.

Another cause of the inflation was paper currency. Not only Congress but each of the thirteen states had its own issue of paper money. There was not enough gold to support this paper blizzard, and the value of the Continental dollar went steadily downward. In 1776, 4 Continental dollars were worth 1 in gold—that is, "hard" money— but in 1779 the ratio was as high as 100 to 1. Desperate,

Congress finally devalued the dollar. They declared that 1 gold dollar was worth 40 Continentals. This step eliminated $200,000,000 from the national debt, but it also made life more difficult for Continental soldiers or other wage earners paid in paper.

Those who had saved their paper money were ruined because their hoard was now worth only one-fortieth of what they thought it had been. If they tried to buy anything with paper money, they were refused by farmers and merchants, who wanted nothing but hard cash or else many times its worth in paper.

Thus, cold, hungry, and penniless, while all around them bloated profiteers made themselves fat and comfortable, the men of the Continental Army endured their fifth winter. As Washington wrote: "The long and great sufferings of this army is unexampled in history."

20

The War Moves South

For five years—since the outbreak of the Revolution—British policy in America had been to crush the rebellion by military operations in the North.

The first objective had been the linkup of two armies on the Hudson. After this was abandoned, by both Sir William Howe's decision to campaign in Pennsylvania and Burgoyne's defeat at Saratoga, the British continued to hope to fight a decisive battle with Washington's army. So long as the colonies could field an army, the rebellion would endure. Conquer that army, however, scatter it—and the Revolution would be at an end.

In the light of this policy, the greatness of George Washington shines even brighter. For five years, supported by a band of devoted officers and some few thousand idealist soldiers, he had preserved this army. He had thwarted British policy. Even more than this, by attracting attention to himself, he had distracted British power from the South, where he had always feared that the Revolution could be lost. Though a Southerner himself, Washington said of the Southern states that "their internal weakness, disaffection, the want of energy, the general languor that has seized the people at large" would make them too weak to defend against British attack.

For this reason, General Washington was very unhappy when, in 1780, the British shifted their line of operations from the North to the South. Since March, 1778, Lord George Germain had been eager to invade the South. He still believed that the South was Toryland. If Georgia and the Carolinas could be conquered, he reasoned, then "all America to the south of the Susquehanna [River] would return to their allegiance," and the North would fall meekly into line.

Sir Henry Clinton shared Germain's conviction. He was especially eager to invade the South after Britain's needs in the war with France and Spain drained off his own strength and made him too weak to meet Washington in decisive battle. Clinton's plan was to use Savannah as a base from which he could conquer the Carolinas. Virginia would be next, after which, his army brought back to strength by Tory recruits, he would march north and defeat Washington. Even if he could not reduce the North, he would at least preserve the South for Britain.

On February 11, with 6,000 regulars and accompanied by Lord Cornwallis, his second-in-command, General Clinton arrived at Charleston. Moving with that slow de-

liberation which was the British army's chief characteristic in America, it took him almost a month to emplace
gun batteries on the Ashley River south of the city. In
that interval, the American commander, General Benjamin Lincoln, reinforced Charleston. Unfortunately,
Lincoln drew all the South Carolina Continentals and
militia to his standard. Thus, the fate of South Carolina
was joined to that of Charleston.

Once Clinton's strength rose to 10,000 men and his
lines were extended to the Cooper River north of the
town, Charleston was caught in a ring of steel. The ring
grew stronger when, under cover of a storm, the British
fleet ran past Fort Moultrie's once-dreaded guns. Then,
the dashing and cruel cavalry leader Colonel Banastre
Tarleton scattered the force of American horse and infantry that held open Lincoln's supply lines on the
Cooper River.

On May 9, 1780, Clinton began bombarding the city.
Although American troops suffered only five casualties,
many fires were started. Frightened, the townspeople
urged General Lincoln to surrender. He did. Surrounded, shot at from land and sea, his supply line cut
off, and both his troops and his citizenry showing little
stomach for battle, he had no alternative. On May 12
Charleston hauled down its flag.

Some 5,000 American soldiers and 3 generals, as well
as 300 cannon, 2 frigates complete with their guns, and
military stores of all descriptions, fell into British hands.
Thus, Charleston became the worst defeat in American
history until the fall of Bataan 162 years later.

Sir Henry Clinton used his victory wisely. Hoping to establish a civil government in South Carolina, he adopted a policy of clemency. Much as the Tories and some of his officers might plead for a patriot bloodbath, he turned instead to granting paroles and pardons. At first, it appeared that Clinton's leniency would be successful. Thousands of rebels took the oath to King George, many of them even volunteering to fight for the crown so long as it would be against only the French or Spanish. Finally, what appeared to be the last vestige of patriot military power in South Carolina appeared to be broken when Colonel Tarleton's legion of mounted Tories defeated American cavalry under Colonel Abraham Buford. Actually, the victory was more of a massacre. With the Americans driven into a mass, their flag of surrender flying and their arms grounded, the Tories fell upon them with cold steel. From this slaughter came the rebel war cry "Tarleton's Quarter!," a byword for the butchery of defenseless men.

"Tarleton's Quarter" also described the hatred which the loyalists of South Carolina bore for their patriot neighbors. Eventually, these Tories shook off Clinton's restraints, and by quenching their thirst for revenge, they wrecked the British commander's program of clemency. And because one atrocity almost always begets another atrocity, civil war was begun in the Carolinas and Georgia as well.

Throughout the region, patriots and Tories were ambushed in cold blood, shot down in the streets, plundered of all their possessions, or even burned alive in their homes. One horrified Continental officer wrote: "I have been so long here amongst the wretched, dam'd and disaffected, I have almost lost every feeling of humanity."

Meanwhile, the patriot reaction made it more difficult for Lord Cornwallis, in charge of military operations, to pacify South Carolina. Guerrilla bands led by men such as Marion and Thomas Sumter were especially vexing to Cornwallis. He did not have enough cavalry to defend against their mounted raids on outposts and his lines of communications. Nevertheless, even with South Carolina far from "conquered," Cornwallis decided to invade North Carolina.

As he did, Congress countered by raising an army to meet the British threat in the South. It numbered about 5,000 men, of whom about 3,000 were militia, and it was commanded by Horatio Gates. Moving south, Gates found his ranks swelled by rebel recruits who had only recently been begging the king's pardon. Now almost twice as strong as Cornwallis, with his Continentals led by the gigantic German Baron de Kalb, he decided to attack the British at Camden.

Unfortunately, before the Americans moved out on the night of August 15, they were fed a poorly cooked meal and a dessert made with a medicinal molasses that acted like a laxative. Many of them were sick and miserable even before they met the enemy.

That meeting was at night, in a pine forest lying between two swamps. At the outset, Tarleton's mounted

Tories charged the American cavalry, forcing them back —only to be driven off themselves by a countercharge. At daylight, however, Cornwallis hurled his light infantry against the American militia on Gates' right. Brandishing their bayonets, cheering, the redcoats put the militia to flight. With the left flank of De Kalb's Continentals now wide open, the redcoats poured through the gap and struck De Kalb's rear.

Rallying his Continentals—men from Maryland and Delaware—the huge nobleman fought stubbornly. Even with his horse shot from under him, his head laid open by a saber, and aware that the militia and General Gates himself had fled, De Kalb fought on. Six hundred Continentals were battling 2,000 British regulars, and at one point they very nearly burst through that ring of steel. But when De Kalb at last sank to the ground, dying from eleven wounds, the Battle of Camden was over.

It ended long before Horatio Gates stopped running. He did not halt until he reached Hillsboro, North Carolina, 240 miles away. As Alexander Hamilton was to quip, it was a fine feat of horsemanship for a man of Gates' age. Thus Gates rode out of the war and into embarrassed retirement. A few days later the British victories at Charleston and Camden were succeeded by Tarlteon's defeat of Francis Marion.

Resistance in South Carolina seemed at an end, and the elated Lord Cornwallis made ready to move north from Camden to invade North Carolina. As he did, he ordered a special elite corps known as Ferguson's Riflemen to cover his left or inland flank.

The commander of this special force of about 800 Tories and 100 regulars was Major Patrick Ferguson, a soldier famous in the British Army both for having invented a breech-loading rifle capable of firing up to six rounds a minute and for the brutal thoroughness with which he carried out his orders. Actually, Ferguson had been a little too brutal and thorough in his scouring of the Carolinas. As a result, he had angered those Scotch-Irish frontiersmen who dwelled across the mountains in what is now Tennessee. Crack shots with their long-barreled rifles, hardy horsemen who could campaign for weeks on a bag of corn, these free spirits were infuriated when Ferguson summoned them to submit to him before he crossed the mountains to destroy them.

Instead, they came to destroy Ferguson. Joined by similar bands of riflemen from Virginia and the Carolinas, led by Colonel John Sevier, Isaac Shelby, Charles McDowell, Benjamin Cleveland, and William Campbell, they numbered about 1,000 when they found Ferguson at King's Mountain.

Major Ferguson now had about 1,200 men, all of them Tories. He had chosen to fight at King's Mountain in western South Carolina because he thought that the summit of that steep and wooded height could be easily defended. It was level, about 500 yards long and 70 to 80 yards wide. At its northeast end where Ferguson established his camp, it broadened to about 120 yards. Here, Ferguson vowed, not even "God Almighty and all the rebels out of Hell" could defeat him.

Undismayed, the rebels began climbing King's Moun-

THE WORLD TURNED UPSIDE DOWN

tain's steep slopes. They were in nine combat parties which formed a huge horseshoe enclosing Ferguson's corps. Reaching the summit, Colonel Campbell cried, "Here they are, boys! Shout like hell, and fight like devils!" At first, however, it was the Tories who fought like devils. Desperate with the knowledge of the treatment they could expect in defeat, they charged the patriots and drove them off.

Taking to the trees, the frontiersmen began picking the Tories off. Meanwhile, they sent party after party against Ferguson's position. As often as they were driven off with the bayonet, they came again—each time whittling Ferguson's strength. Throughout, the deadly rifle fire from the treetops took its toll. At last, the Tories thought their cause was hopeless. Twice they raised white flags into the air, and each time the doughty Patrick Ferguson cut them down. But the ring drew tighter, ever tighter, and as Ferguson tried to cut his way through it, he was shot dying from his horse.

Now the rebels charged. Crying, "Buford! Buford! Tarleton's Quarter!," they drove the Tories into a huddled, whimpering mass and began their own slaughter of revenge. "For God's sake, quit!" Colonel Campbell cried, riding among them. "It's murder to shoot any more!" It was indeed, but even so, nine Tories believed to have been in the massacre of Buford's men were executed after the battle. The remaining prisoners were forced to march two days without food.

Such were the hatreds that divided the South, and yet King's Mountain, dishonored though it was by such brutal behavior, was a signal victory. Only 200 of Ferguson's men sent out earlier to forage had escaped death or capture. And once Lord Cornwallis heard of the defeat, he dropped his invasion of North Carolina and began to withdraw to the south.

21

Tale of a Traitor

Although battle had erupted briskly and bloodily in
the South, the war in the North had come almost to a
standstill.

Except for the Southern civil war and the campaigns of
Cornwallis in the Carolinas, it appeared that the people
of the United States during the year 1780 had ceased to
care about the Revolution. Congress was bankrupt and
the country so indifferent to Washington's calls for recruits that he despaired of ever going back into action
again.

But then, in July, some 5,000 French soldiers under
the veteran commander Comte de Rochambeau began
landing unopposed at the former British bastion in Newport. Even though many patriot leaders resented the
presence of French troops on American soil, preferring to

win their liberty through their own arms, General Washington was delighted. More than anyone else, he realized the value of French help, and he hoped also that their support would revive drooping American spirits.

Unfortunately, this did not happen. Even though Americans resented the appearance of the white-coated Bourbon soldiers, insisting that all they sought from France was supplies, not men, Washington's ranks remained thin. Then, to his intense dismay, a British fleet bottled up De Rochambeau's troops in Newport, also blockading another 5,000 soldiers at the French seaport of Brest.

For George Washington, there would be no campaign of 1780. And so, with that undying faith in ultimate victory which was one of his most valuable traits, Washington decided to confer with Comte de Rochambeau on a plan for 1781. So he went to New London, Connecticut, confident that Clinton, who had returned to New York City, would make no campaign either. Accordingly, no special precautions were taken in the American outposts to guard against such an event. Certainly there were none at West Point, the vital new American fort guarding the Hudson, now commanded by Benedict Arnold.

Having been crippled by his wound at Saratoga, Benedict Arnold had been forced to give up field command and to accept less active duties. Thus, he became the military commander of Philadelphia.

Here, in "the Paris of America," General Arnold became one of the gayest of the gay. Establishing himself in the splendid mansion once occupied by Sir William Howe, Arnold dashed about the city in a handsome coach-and-four, with servants in livery to drive him or to open doors for him and his guests.

Benedict Arnold loved to entertain, especially pretty young women such as beautiful Peggy Shippen, the eighteen-year-old daughter of a wealthy Tory merchant. Peggy had once been the darling of Philadelphia social life when it was conducted under the paternal eye of General Howe. Only an accident kept her off the rebel blacklist.

When Sir William Howe was leaving Philadelphia, a gala farewell was held in his honor. Because the young girls were supposed to wear Turkish bloomers at the party, Peggy Shippen's father would not let her attend. And because nonattendance at that fete was made the test of loyalty to the Revolution, Peggy Shippen was acceptable to the Americans. Thus, she met and eventually married the dashing Major General Benedict Arnold.

At once, Arnold's expenses soared. Not content with his old house for his beautiful young bride, he bought Mount Pleasant, a fine estate on the Schuylkill River. There the newlyweds indulged each other in all their expensive tastes. As a result, Benedict Arnold found himself in great need of funds.

In defense of Benedict Arnold, it has been observed that his military genius—and he was probably the most capable of all American field commanders—had been ignored by the people. This, and the fact that Congress had repeatedly snubbed him, it is argued, had embittered

Arnold. Moreover, he was awaiting court-martial on charges of having misused public property. Thus, the argument runs, Arnold's pride was deeply wounded, and in resentment he turned to lining his own pockets just like the "patriot" profiteers around him.

Although there is much truth in these claims, the fact remains that Arnold's high style of living made it necessary for him to make money. The only way he knew how was by graft, by the use of his official position to make deals or to seize property left behind by fugitive loyalists. But he never made enough money, so, when his marriage to Peggy Shippen put him in need of more, he turned in his resentment to dealing with the enemy.

Through the offices of a china dealer named Joseph Stansbury, he opened correspondence with Major John André, now the chief of British intelligence in New York, but once the friend of Arnold's wife. That was in May, 1779, and André dropped the correspondence in disgust after he discovered that Arnold's only purpose in betraying the rebel cause was to be paid for doing it.

In 1780 a court-martial found Benedict Arnold guilty of the old charges. He was sentenced to be publicly rebuked by Washington, and the American commander carried out the sentence. More embittered than before, Arnold renewed his advances to André, this time sending along top-secret documents to verify both his high position and his intentions. Now André and Sir Henry Clinton were interested. Shortly afterward they were overjoyed to learn that Major General Benedict Arnold had been named commander of West Point.

Here was the key to the Hudson. British possession of it might revive the old strategy of cutting off New England. On Clinton's orders André began to bargain with Arnold for the betrayal of West Point. Here Arnold showed his true character. Nothing was said, as he maintained later, about his fearing that France would take power in America, replacing its Protestant faith with Roman Catholicism. All he wanted was gold—so much for the fort, so much for every betrayed soldier—in all, £10,000 plus a general's commission.

Clinton agreed, and sent Major André, his most trusted aide, up the Hudson to close the deal. Sailing upriver in the sloop of war *Vulture*, André met Arnold on the west shore below Haverstraw. While the two conferred, American gun batteries opened fire on *Vulture* and drove her downriver.

André was stranded. Although Clinton had warned him against traveling by land and had instructed him to wear his uniform at all times, he allowed Arnold to persuade him to return on foot and to wear civilian clothes. Worse, he also ignored Clinton's warning against carrying incriminating documents. Again at Arnold's urging, he put evidence of the planned betrayal in his stockings. Then André departed. Two days later, on September 23, he was captured in Tarrytown. The papers in his stockings were found.

General Washington was notified. Enraged, he moved immediately to take Arnold prisoner. But the traitor had been warned by a bumbling, though innocent, American officer. A bare hour before Washington arrived at the fort, Arnold mounted his horse, bade his wife and child farewell—and galloped away for his barge moored on the Hudson. Rowed to the *Vulture*, he calmly surrendered his rowers to the skipper.

Arnold's next service to his new masters was to identify almost every American spy in New York City, thus shutting off Washington's flow of information and placing the person and property of his former countrymen in jeopardy. After that, he settled down to bargain with Clinton. Even though he had failed to betray West Point, he still demanded his £10,000. He claimed that if the British were defeated, the patriots would seize property he owned which was worth at least that much. In the end, Clinton agreed to pay him £6,315, together with a general's commission, an annual pension of £500 for his wife, and £100 for each of his children. After his service in the South and later against the French, the crown also granted Arnold 13,000 acres of land in what is now the Canadian province of Ontario.

Sir Henry Clinton had paid his traitor well. But he could do little to save his dearest friend, Major John André. Because the British officer had been captured in civilian clothes and because of the nature of his dealings with Arnold, Washington had ordered André hanged as a spy. Clinton pleaded eloquently for his life. But Washington, remembering what Howe had done to Nathan Hale, could not be moved.

Major André went to his death proudly. Determined to show the rebels how an English gentleman could die, he put on full regimentals and strode to the gallows with a cheerful face. There he courteously helped the hang-man adjust the noose around his neck and tied the hand-kerchief around his eyes himself.

Many of the Americans who saw him die wept openly. Every last man would have preferred to see Benedict Arnold in his place.

22

"And Fight Again"

Although the treason of Benedict Arnold came as a fitting climax to the black year of 1780, it had little effect on the war itself. Inflation and a worthless currency were of far graver consequences.

By mid-1780 the Continental dollar was worth no more than a penny. Congress, recognizing reality, adopted the barter system. It also called upon the thirteen states to supply the Continental Army, not by paying money, but by providing goods.

As a result, the army's plight worsened. "New" clothing and "prime" steers delivered to the depots turned out to be worn-out garments and runt cattle. Even the shabby goods deposited there failed to reach the troops, if only because Congress had provided no means of delivering them.

So the soldiers continued to go hungry and half-naked, while all around them the countryside prospered. At last their patience gave way. In 1780 the outraged, frustrated troops of the Pennsylvania Line began to plunder civilians. They fell upon the countryside with a savagery rivaling the atrocious conduct of the Hessians. Although many of them were punished, the whip was no solution to the problem. Food and clothing and good hard cash were the answer, and when these were not forthcoming, a spirit of rebellion took hold of the soldiers.

On New Year's Day, 1781, the men of the Pennsylvania Line quartered in Morristown mutinied. Drunk with a New Year's issue of rum, they fell upon their officers, killed three, and injured many others. Fearing that they might go over to the British, General Wayne personally blocked the road to New York City. The men fired shots over his head, but when he refused to budge, they turned and marched south to Princeton.

Actually, the Pennsylvania soldiers had no intention of betraying the Revolution. They wanted only what they rarely received—fair treatment. At Princeton, under their sergeants, they maintained the strictest discipline. They even seized two spies whom Clinton had planted among them and handed them over for trial and execution. Then they marched to Trenton, where they were met by Joseph Reed, president of the Pennsylvania Council.

General Washington, meanwhile, was in a dilemma. He hoped to prevent the mutiny from spreading, but if he used force to quell it, it might anger the remaining units of the Continental Army. In the end, he promised the Pennsylvanians part of the back pay due them and discharged those who claimed their enlistments were up. In this way, the problem was solved.

But then the smaller New Jersey Line stationed at Pompton also mutinied. Now Washington was ruthless. He ordered General Robert Howe and a powerful force of New England Continentals to Pompton. There the Jerseyans were surrounded in their huts and forced to parade without arms. Singling out the ringleaders, General Howe commanded twelve of them to shoot the two most guilty ones, and in that way the New Jersey mutiny was crushed.

As George Washington knew, however, only an upturn in military fortunes could keep his unhappy army from falling apart.

The good news that revived the failing spirits of the patriots came from the South. There Nathanael Greene had succeeded the retired Horatio Gates as commander of the Southern army. Taking charge in Charlotte, Greene immediately realized that the 3,000 ragged soldiers he commanded were no match for Cornwallis' 4,000 regulars. But he could not retreat and thus risk losing the entire South. So he decided to conduct an irregular war.

This is a war of attrition, the type of hit-and-run warfare that whittles the enemy's strength, drains off his supplies, and destroys his will to fight. General Greene's plan was to operate against the British flanks with two main columns, while the irregular leaders, Marion and Sumter, nibbled on his rear. The Americans would live off the country and depend on their knowledge of the terrain and their mobility to elude the road-bound, equipment-heavy British.

One of the main columns under Isaac Huger, accompanied by Greene, would move east from Charlotte, while the other under Daniel Morgan would march west. Thus, if Cornwallis moved to his right to intercept Greene, he would unmask the towns of Ninety-Six and Camden to Morgan. If he struck to his left, he would leave Charleston open to Greene. Realizing this, Cornwallis decided to divide his own forces. While he stayed in the east watching Greene, Banastre Tarleton went riding to the west to destroy Morgan. On January 17, 1781, Tarleton and Morgan met at Cowpens.

Daniel Morgan's decision to fight at Cowpens was based on his distrust of his militia. Like most veteran commanders, he agreed with Washington's remark that the militia were "useless hands and mouths" who "consume your provisions, exhaust your stores and leave you at the critical moment." So Morgan chose to fight with the Broad River at his back and swamps on either flank. Unable to run, he said later, the militia would have to stand.

To his front he placed 150 picked riflemen in a skirmish line. About 150 yards farther back were his militia —300 men under Andrew Pickens—and back another 150 yards on a hilltop was his main body of 400 Continentals under John Howard. Still farther back, behind another hill, was his cavalry—100 horsemen led by portly William Washington, the officer who was wounded at Trenton.

Morgan ordered his sharpshooters up front not to fire until Tarleton's cavalrymen were within fifty yards and then to pick off the officers. After two volleys, they were to fall back. Then the militia were to fire two volleys, before retiring behind the first hill to be held as a reserve. Morgan promised the militia that they would be in no danger, and he also wisely informed every man of the movements he planned, so that no one would become upset by the sudden withdrawals.

As Morgan expected, the impetuous Tarleton sent his Tory cavalry charging forward. American rifles blazed, fifteen horsemen fell, and the Tory horsemen fled the field for good. Nevertheless, the main British line surged forward. On either flank were British dragoons, or mounted marksmen. To Morgan's delight, the militia held their ground, firing, reloading, and firing again before taking flight as instructed. Thinking that they had broken the Americans, the British dragoons charged. And then—out of nowhere, it seemed—Washington's riders came thundering out of the American right rear. They fell on the startled dragoons and routed them. Meanwhile, the militia gained the safety of the hill and re-formed.

Still, the British infantry came on. Tarleton extended his left flank, trying to get around the Continentals. Howard gave the order for his right-hand company to form a right angle to the main line to blunt the British maneuver. By mistake, the company marched to the rear, and the entire main line followed suit.

Thunderstruck, Morgan rushed up to Howard, crying, "What is this retreat?"

"A change of position to save my right flank," Howard yelled.

"Are you beaten?" Morgan shouted, and Howard shot back scornfully: "Do men who march like that look as though they were beaten?" Satisfied, Morgan found Howard's Continentals a second position between the two hills.

In the meantime, Tarleton, believing he had the Americans on the run, pressed forward. So eager were his men for the kill that they broke ranks and charged. With that, William Washington's horsemen, returning from the pursuit of the routed dragoons, saw the British confusion and struck and broke their flank and rear.

That was the end of the Battle of Cowpens. Tarleton had suffered his first defeat, a crushing one in which he lost nine-tenths of his command. Worse for Lord Cornwallis, the loss at Cowpens deprived him of the light troops he needed for his invasion of North Carolina. Yet Cornwallis did not abandon his campaign. He realized that British defeats at King's Mountain and Cowpens had only been possible because Virginia and North Carolina remained in rebel hands. So long as these two states held out, he could not even be sure of South Carolina and Georgia.

Thus, Lord Cornwallis set himself to the destruction

of Nathanael Greene's army. First, he tried to cut off Morgan, but the "Old Wagoner" eluded him and joined forces with Greene. Together, they withdrew into Virginia. Cornwallis pursued, and Greene came south to meet him at Guilford Courthouse in North Carolina. There, though outnumbering the enemy 4,400 to 1,800, Greene was defeated. But he had inflicted more losses on the British, just as he planned.

Next, Greene met the British under Lord Rawdon at Hobkirk's Hill. Once again, he was defeated—but not crushed. Meanwhile, Marion cut Rawdon's line of communications, and the British were forced to withdraw. That gave Greene the opportunity to take his army to the High Hills of Santee to rest until the scorching heat of the summer had ended. Then Greene marched south again. On September 8, 1781, he met the British at Eutaw Springs, South Carolina. There, for the first time, it appeared that he would be the victor. His men drove the enemy from the field and might have finished them, had they not stopped to consume supplies of rum found in the British camp. Before Greene could restore discipline, the re-formed British counterattacked and drove him off.

Nevertheless, Nathanael Greene had successfully carried out his strategy. As he had written to a friend: "We fight, get beat, rise, and fight again." By taking tactical loss after tactical loss, he had scored a strategic victory. Even as Greene drove deeper south, Cornwallis, in late May, 1781, decided to abandon the state of South Carolina and to carry the war to Virginia instead.

23

The World Turned Upside Down

In the shifting tides of British policy, Virginia had become the state in which the rebellion would be crushed. Because the Old Dominion gave such valuable support to the Revolution by exchanging its tobacco for military supplies, the British believed they could strangle the patriot economy there.

All that was needed, they thought, was to establish a blockade. With a naval station set up on Chesapeake Bay, the port of Baltimore would be closed to rebel shipping and Virginia's tobacco would be left to rot in warehouses.

As early as 1779, a base was set up at Portsmouth, and American shipping in the Chesapeake was bottled up. Moving with a surprising ease that embarrassed that doughty Virginian George Washington, the British began to plunder his home state. Then, probably because

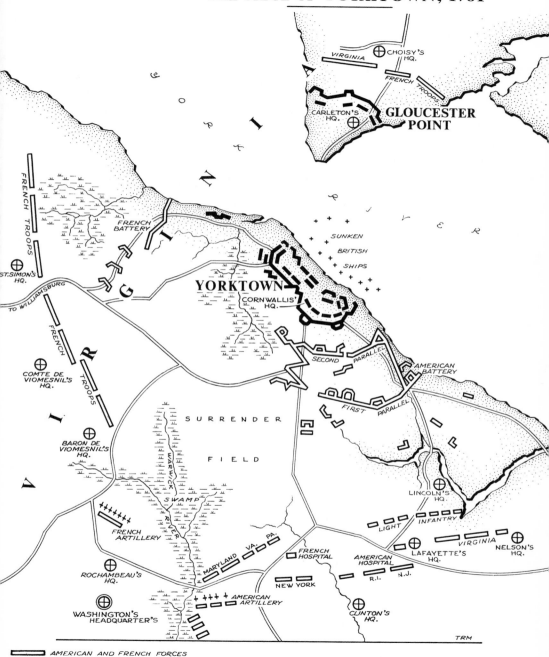

THE SIEGE OF **YORKTOWN, 1781**

VIRGINIA

CHOISY'S HQ.

FRENCH TROOPS

CARLETON'S HQ.

GLOUCESTER POINT

YORK RIVER

FRENCH TROOPS

FRENCH BATTERY

ST. SIMON'S HQ.

TO WILLIAMSBURG

FRENCH TROOPS

COMTE DE VIOMESNIL'S HQ.

BARON DE VIOMESNIL'S HQ.

FRENCH ARTILLERY

ROCHAMBEAU'S HQ.

WASHINGTON'S HEADQUARTER'S

V I R G I N I A

SUNKEN BRITISH SHIPS

YORKTOWN

CORNWALLIS' HQ.

SECOND PARALLEL

AMERICAN BATTERY

FIRST PARALLEL

SURRENDER FIELD

WARWICK RIVER

SWAMP

MARYLAND VA. PA.

FRENCH HOSPITAL

NEW YORK

AMERICAN ARTILLERY

AMERICAN HOSPITAL

R.I.   N.J.

CLINTON'S HQ.

LINCOLN'S HQ.

LIGHT INFANTRY

LAFAYETTE'S HQ.

VIRGINIA

NELSON'S HQ.

TRM

AMERICAN AND FRENCH FORCES

BRITISH DEFENSE POSITIONS

1500 YARDS

of the distraction of the war with France and Spain, Britain neglected Virginia for almost two years. Troops needed for Cornwallis' campaigns in the Carolinas were withdrawn from Portsmouth, and the base was abandoned.

In late 1780, however, the British returned—commanded by Brigadier General Benedict Arnold. With customary thoroughness "the Arch-Traitor and Patricide" made a smoking hell of the Old Dominion. He sent home enough personal plunder to satisfy even his own dreams of avarice while putting huge quantities of tobacco to the torch, burning plantations, and carrying off hundreds of Negro slaves. Virginia hardly lifted a finger to stop him, and he burned and plundered Richmond at his leisure after forcing Governor Thomas Jefferson, the House of Burgesses, and most of the townspeople to flee for their lives.

Because Arnold served his new masters so well in Virginia, and because the state did next to nothing to capture and hang him, the Old Dominion fell out of favor with the other states. One Virginia officer complained that his homeland was "so reproached by everybody, that it is almost dishonorable to be a Virginian."

General Washington was also dismayed. Nevertheless, he refused to go south himself. He had no intention of dividing his army and risk being gobbled up in chunks. Instead, he sent the Marquis de Lafayette to Virginia with orders to take Arnold captive. Before Lafayette arrived, 4,000 Virginia militia besieged Arnold in Portsmouth, while a French fleet blockaded the Chesapeake.

The "Arch-Traitor" appeared trapped, until a British fleet drove the French back to Newport, Rhode Island, thus uncorking Arnold.

Now Sir Henry Clinton sent reinforcements into Virginia, placing General William Phillips in command. Arnold, to Virginia's intense relief, returned north, where he burned his hometown of New London "by accident." In all, when Cornwallis arrived in Virginia in the summer of 1781, he had a total of about 7,000 men to command.

In New York, meanwhile, Sir Henry Clinton had intercepted letters from Washington and Comte de Rochambeau. They indicated that an attack on New York City was being prepared. Alarmed, Clinton ordered Cornwallis to send him 3,000 men.

Marching to Portsmouth to embark the troops, the British commander was attacked at Green Springs by Lafayette. Anxious as ever to catch "the boy," Cornwallis defeated the Americans but could not crush them. That was on July 6, 1781. Thereafter, Clinton sent Cornwallis a stream of conflicting orders which finally concluded by instructing him to keep all his troops if he thought he needed them.

Lord Cornwallis thought he did. In August, 1781, he led them into summer quarters at the little tobacco port of Yorktown.

During the previous July, Washington and De Rochambeau, each with about 5,000 men, had joined forces. Then they probed New York City, where they hoped to strike Clinton. To Washington's intense disappointment, they found Clinton much too strong to be attacked. For the first time during the war, the American commander began to consider a campaign in the South. De Rochambeau encouraged him, if only because he had privately advised Admiral de Grasse that the Chesapeake would offer the best opportunities for his fleet. On August 14, Washington was delighted to hear that De Grasse with twenty-eight ships of the line and 4,000 men had left the West Indies for Chesapeake Bay. At once the American saw the chance to trap Cornwallis, and he immediately wrote to Lafayette to keep the British commander cooped up in Yorktown. Admiral de Barras was ordered to take De Rochambeau's artillery from Newport to the Chesapeake.

The next step was to convince Clinton that the Franco-American blow would be aimed at him. Roads toward Staten Island were improved to create the impression that an assault would be launched overwater from there. Field ovens were built in Chatham, New Jersey. Leaving 3,000 men above New York to distract Clinton, Washington marched slowly into New Jersey with the remaining 2,000. All the French followed. It appeared to Clinton that they were bound for Sandy Hook.

On August 30, the patriots and their French allies stepped up the marching pace and turned their faces south toward Yorktown.

Aware that De Grasse had sailed for the Chesapeake, Britain's Admiral Sir Samuel Hood left the West Indies in pursuit with fourteen "liners." Taking the direct route, while De Grasse sailed a longer one, he arrived in the Chesapeake ahead of the Frenchman. Looking inside the bay, finding no one, Admiral Hood set sail for New York. There he joined Admiral Samuel Graves with five liners.

A cautious, indecisive commander, Graves was nevertheless senior to Hood, and he took command of the combined fleet, sailing south again in hopes of intercepting Admiral de Barras with De Rochambeau's artillery. Arriving off the Chesapeake, he was astonished to find De Grasse inside with a superior fleet.

Quickly clearing his decks for battle, the Frenchman made for the open sea, where his superior firepower drove the English away. Then De Grasse kept at sea for five more days, luring Graves away from the Chesapeake so that De Barras might safely slip inside with De Rochambeau's artillery. After De Barras did enter the bay, De Grasse joined him and Admiral Graves sailed north again.

In New York City, meanwhile, a horrified Sir Henry Clinton realized that Washington and De Rochambeau were making for Yorktown and Lord Cornwallis. Unable to overtake them by land, he was compelled to await the arrival of the British fleet under Graves.

The march from New Jersey to Yorktown was a grueling ordeal. Although Washington's artillery and some of his Continentals were able to sail down the Chesapeake from Head of Elk, most of the American and French troops had to go by land. En route, the French passed through Philadelphia, saluting Congress as a crowned head and deeply impressing the Americans with their smart military appearance. Later these white-coated soldiers so impressed Anthony Wayne that he remarked, "The French are the finest body of troops that I ever viewed."

But if the presence of French soldiers could so reassure most Americans, the apparent absence of French sailors continued to disturb George Washington. All the way south, he was troubled, firing off letter after letter to Lafayette, asking where De Grasse was. Washington feared that the British fleet might get to the Chesapeake first and relieve Cornwallis. But then, riding into the Franco-American camp at Yorktown, he was greeted by Lafayette, who rushed up to embrace his chief and to tell him that De Grasse held the Chesapeake with a powerful fleet.

General Washington swung his hat wildly. Cornwallis was caught! The French had already put nearly 4,000 more soldiers ashore! Finding the Comte de Rochambeau, Washington embraced him. Everywhere in the Franco-American camp there were cheers. To the Americans' surprise, some of the French officers kissed them. Yet everyone knew, as one Virginia general remarked, "we have got him handsomely in a pudding bag."

Lord Cornwallis knew it, too. He had realized he was trapped the moment he saw the sun-dappled sails of his enemy. Situated as he was, on the tip of a peninsula almost surrounded by water, he was nailed between an allied army to his front and the French fleet at his back. So he decided to make a stand at Yorktown, strengthening his fortifications with the aid of 2,000 black slaves who had fled to his camp. In the meantime, he hoped, Sir Henry Clinton and the British fleet would come to his relief.

Clinton worked feverishly to organize a rescue expedition. But he had to dance in attendance on the admirals. With only twenty-three ships to match against De Grasse's thirty-seven, the navy was inclined to give up on Cornwallis. Besides, many of the British ships were badly in need of repairs. And there were grave shortages of materials in the New York dockyards. Nevertheless, Clinton urged them to get busy. And then, to his intense dismay, Prince William, the son of King George III, arrived in New York for a visit. Two valuable days had to be wasted on entertaining the prince. And September was almost gone. . . .

On September 30, to General Washington's astonishment and pleasure, Cornwallis abandoned his outer works at Gloucester. As he explained later, he had received word from Clinton that help was on the way. So he was falling back on Yorktown to concentrate. Even so, the Franco-Americans at once occupied the abandoned positions and put artillery there.

On October 9 a French battery opened fire on Yorktown. Then an American battery roared into life, with George Washington firing the first shot. On the following night larger field pieces began to fire. Three British ships were destroyed. Cornwallis' camp at Yorktown began to quiver and fall apart. In all, fifty-two guns were battering the British positions. Cornwallis wrote to Clinton:

"We have lost about seventy of our men and many of our works are considerably damaged; with such works on disadvantageous ground against so powerful an attack we cannot hope to make a very long resistance. P.S. 5 P.M. Since my letter was written (at 12 M) we have lost thirty men. . . . We continue to lose men very fast."

Clinton was beside himself. He had put 7,000 men aboard transports two weeks before the fleet was to sail. October 5—the sailing date—came and went with the fleet still at anchor. Another week ticked away. Clinton was frantic. Finally, on October 17, the ships set sail. But the wind and tides were against them. Two more days passed, and on October 19 the rescue armada stood out to the open sea.

Long before then, the Franco-Americans had inched their first trench to within 300 yards of the British positions. Fire from British redoubts struck the working parties, and Washington ordered the enemy strongpoint taken. On the left, the French went forward in a stirring charge, climbing the parapet with shouts of "Long live the king!" There the Hessian and British troops surrendered. On the right the Americans surged forward behind Alexander Hamilton. They drove in with the bayonet.

General Washington watched the attacks go forward, ignoring the storm of British fire that swept the field.

"Sir," his aide said, "you are too much exposed here. Had you not better step a little back?"

"Colonel Cobb," Washington replied evenly, "if you are afraid, you have liberty to step back."

Then the second British position fell, the siege trench was completed, and a second one was begun. Alarmed, Cornwallis ordered a party of 350 soldiers to destroy the gun batteries in the trench. Sallying out in a brave charge, the British succeeded in taking and spiking some of the guns but were eventually driven off.

The date was October 16, and that same midnight Cornwallis began embarking his troops on transports in the York River. He hoped to escape across the river through Gloucester. But a violent storm forced him to cancel the operation.

On the following day, two days before Clinton's rescue fleet finally upped anchor, the combined Franco-American batteries began battering Yorktown. There was no answering British fire. Instead, a drummer boy marched bravely onto a parapet and began to beat a parley. The allied guns fell silent. A British officer strode stiffly forward to be blindfolded and led to General Washington.

The officer asked for a 24-hour armistice, but Washington, aware that Cornwallis was playing for time, granted him only two. Returning to the allied camp, the officer brought Cornwallis' surrender terms. They asked that the British army be paroled to Britain. Washington refused, insisting that they surrender as prisoners of war— and Cornwallis agreed.

It was at noon of October 19 that the surrender ceremony took place. On the right were the French, smart in their white regimentals, their bands playing gaily. On the left were the Americans, first the Continentals in blue and buff, but behind them the ragged, lean militia, many of them in brown hunting shirts. General Washington, mounted on a great bay horse, was in front of them, with Generals Wayne and Von Steuben. Opposite Washington, also mounted, were De Rochambeau and De Barras.

Yorktown's main sally port flew open. An officer rode out. To everyone's surprise, it was not Lord Cornwallis, but Brigadier General Charles O'Hara. Pleading illness, Cornwallis had had the bad grace to send a deputy to surrender. Uneasy, General O'Hara approached De Rochambeau, but the count's eyes moved toward Washington. O'Hara rode up to the American, but Washington would not receive Cornwallis' sword. If Cornwallis could send a deputy, then Washington would have a deputy accept his surrender, and he indicated Brigadier General Benjamin Lincoln. Embarrassed, O'Hara gave Lincoln his chief's sword. Lincoln at once returned it and called for the surrender to begin.

First to come out were the Hessians, brisk and military in their blue and green uniforms. Eyes straight ahead, they quickly stacked arms. To many of them, it meant that this miserable war was at last over and they could go home to Germany. Next were the red-coated British— stiff, sullen, some of them weeping, their eyes kept carefully away from the detestable rebels and focused on the French. But Lafayette ordered his bands to play "Yankee

Doodle," reminding the British of the American presence.

Now the British arms went crashing down. Drummer boys smashed their drums; soldiers broke their musket butts. Suddenly, many of the rebels began to jeer. They had beaten the British, and they would not take their contempt. But then, over the cursing of the redcoats and the taunts of the rebels, there came the squealing notes of the British band playing "The World Turned Upside Down."

It was true. The world had somersaulted. At Yorktown, the conclusive battle of the Revolution, "a new order of things" was born. Although there was to be another year of sparring battle, most of it on the western borders, there would be no more major campaigns. And although it would not be until September 3, 1783, that the signing of the Peace of Paris brought the war to a formal close, for all practical purposes it had ended at Yorktown on October 19, 1781.

Lord North was well aware of this. When he received the news of Cornwallis' surrender, he actually staggered and threw his arms wide.

"Oh, God!" he cried. "It is all over!"

Index

The Author

Robert Leckie has written a score of books, most of them on military history, besides many articles on war for national magazines. Born in Philadelphia, he grew up in Rutherford, New Jersey, where his writing career began as a sixteen-year-old sportswriter for *The Record* of Bergen County. In World War II he was wounded and decorated during nearly three years of service with the First Marine Division in the Pacific. His *Conflict: The History of the Korean War*, published by Putnam's, has been called the best military history of that war. Mr. Leckie, his wife, and three children now live in Mountain Lakes, New Jersey.